My
Granny Square
Wardrobe

Dedication

For Dad, who made me believe
anything is possible.

Acknowledgements

Firstly, I would like to thank my lovely husband, Jon, children, Jake, Ana, Leo and Olive, and the rest of my family who have listened patiently, supported me throughout the process and even modelled the garments on occasion!

I also need to thank my fabulous friends – Terri-Anne Perkins and Debs Berry who I have come to call my 'crochet wing women'. They have shared my enthusiasm and passion for the book since the idea was born. They have proofread, tested and edited many of the patterns in the book, but most importantly have been a source of endless encouragement and I consider myself lucky to call them my friends.

I must also thank the wider crochet community. I started crochet as a hobby for myself, but what I didn't realize was that it would introduce me to a wonderful community of fellow crochet lovers. When I began working on the designs for the book I put a call out on social media asking for pattern testers. I was wowed by the response – people from all over the country have given up their time to test the patterns and make samples, many of which have been photographed for the book. So, thank you to: Amanda Price, Clare Goodman, Ella Mae Breakspear, Emma McDougall, Julie Ward, Lynda Little, Melanee Livesey, Natalie Floyd, Sam Hannaby, Sandra Williams, Sian Maguire and Teresa Streeter – I couldn't have done it without you!

Finally, I would like to thank the wonderful team at Search Press who have taken my dream and made it reality. Thanks especially to Carrie Baker, my editor. And thank you to the fabulous team on the model photoshoot: Leanne Jade (photographer), Claire Montgomerie (stylist), Julia Edwards (makeup artist), Louisa Roberts-West (model), Joy-Ann White (model) and Emily Toledo (model).

Suppliers

Thank you to www.woolwarehouse.co.uk, King Cole and Wendy Yarns who kindly provided yarn for me to use for the projects in the book.

SAM SABIDO

My Granny Square Wardrobe

Stunning designs to crochet and wear

SEARCH PRESS

Contents

Projects:

WINTER'S DAY SCARF 14

WINTER'S DAY HAT 18

FEEL THE MAGIC BAG 22

**A HUG FROM GRANNY
COCOON CARDIGAN 26**

MEMORY LANE JACKET 30

WOODSTOCK DUNGAREES 36

WALK IN THE PARK PONCHO 44

COLOUR FADE JUMPER 52

FEELING GROOVY DRESS 64

FRESH AS A DAISY VEST 72

FRESH AS A DAISY SHORTS 78

FEEL THE SUNSHINE SHRUG 84

CAREFREE COATIGAN 94

**HAPPY SUNFLOWER
CARDIGAN 102**

STARRY NIGHT JUMPER 112

Introduction

Hi, I'm Sam, I live in a small town in the Chilterns, UK, with my husband, four children, three chickens, cat and a menagerie of other animals. I love collecting vintage crockery and doing anything crafty.

I started crocheting when I was diagnosed with postnatal depression and my health visitor suggested learning a new hobby to give me time for myself. I fell in love with crochet and haven't looked back! At the time I was a qualified primary school teacher but after I had my fourth child I established my own business teaching and designing crochet. Crochet has changed my life – it has given me space to be me and it has introduced me to a wonderful community of like-minded people. It has also given me confidence in myself and the courage to express my creativity.

I have worked on many crochet projects over the years, but the granny square is my all-time favourite. I love the mindfulness that comes with working on a granny square. The repetitive nature of the pattern is comforting and reassuring. And, as a lover of vintage style, granny squares feel nostalgic yet timeless. They provide an exciting opportunity to have fun with colour and they make a great stash buster. You can be as colourful or as muted as you like, and each project will look different depending on which colour palette you choose.

Finally, and most importantly, granny squares provide a straightforward and fun starting point for making crochet garments!

How to use this book

In this book I will take you through the process of making garments using granny squares. Many people tell me they have made blankets and shawls but haven't felt ready to progress onto making clothes. With this book I hope to give you the confidence to crochet your own clothing.

The patterns are organized in a progressive order from straightforward to more complex. With each pattern I add a new skill, so if you would like to treat the book as a learning process you can work through the projects in order. However, you may also choose to dip in and out. If you are new to making garments I would suggest starting with one of the earlier patterns in the book. If you are a more experienced crocheter you can choose to start wherever you like. I am hoping that you will revisit the book time and time again!

Secrets for success

Before you start, I would like to share some of my secrets for success when making crochet clothing.

TAKE MEASUREMENTS

I highly recommend measuring yourself (or the person you are making the garment for) with a tape measure before you start, so that you can choose which size to make from the size charts provided within each project.

CONSIDER THE FIT YOU WOULD LIKE

Above each size chart I have provided an indication of the type of fit that the garment is designed to have. These range from fitted to oversized and they reflect the amount of ease I have allowed. Once you have taken your body measurements, you can choose the type of fit you would like and may want to make a smaller or larger size to alter how the garment fits. For example, the shorts (see page 78) are designed to be fitted so if you would like a loose fit make a size bigger than your measurements.

Skin tight = negative ease
The finished garment is smaller than the actual measurements.

Fitted = zero ease
The finished garment is the same as actual measurements.

Loose = around 4in (10cm) ease
The finished garment is slightly larger than actual size.

Oversized = 6–8in (15–20cm) ease
The finished garment is oversized.

CHOOSING YOUR YARN

For each of the projects in the book I have specified the brand of yarn that I have used. It is easy to substitute this for a different yarn (or even to use your stash) and I have provided some guidance on how to do so on page 124.

MEASURE YOUR GAUGE (TENSION)

For every design I have provided a gauge (tension) size. This is so that you can check that your gauge is the correct size to obtain the final garment size. If your gauge swatch is more than ¼in (1cm) larger, go down a hook size, if it's more than ¼in (1cm) smaller, go up a hook size and try again.

TRY ON AS YOU GO ALONG

It is really helpful to try on the garment as you make it. Before final assembly you can use stitch markers, pins or large stitches (basting/tacking stitches) to hold it together so that you can try it on. This gives you the opportunity to make alterations for sizes such as the neck hole, armhole depth, sleeve length and overall length before you assemble (depending on pattern).

WEAVE IN THE ENDS WELL

This is super important! Weave in to the point that you are absolutely sure and then weave some more! My tip would be to thread back and forth several times trying to actually break through the yarn fibres as you go. You will feel the yarn thickening in this area which means that it has felted together therefore making it very secure.

HAND WASH OR MACHINE WASH?

If you are confident that you have woven your ends in securely you should be able to machine wash your garment. However you may like to put it in a pillowcase or something similar to protect it from the spin and always wash on the delicate cycle. If in doubt, hand wash!

BLOCK YOUR WORK!

The term 'blocking' refers to dampening and shaping your work. Blocking your squares as you finish them gives them a nice, neat finish and a consistent shape. You can spray with water, starch or even wash them and then shape them onto a blocking board (left) or pin to a towel on your ironing board and allow them to air dry. You can block your finished garment in the same way and also after washing it to keep the shape.

Using a blocking board can make a big difference to your finished granny squares.

Working with charts

I have included symbol charts throughout the book, such as the one below. As you work through the written pattern you might find it useful to refer to the symbol chart for clarification. You can find a key to the chart symbols opposite, and also on the inside front cover flap for easy reference while you work.

Left-handed working

The charts and photographs throughout this book are right-handed. If you are left-handed, when working the granny squares you will work in the opposite direction – your stitches will be worked clockwise rather than anti-clockwise. If you would like to use the charts in the book you could hold a mirror beside the images and follow the image in the reflection.

Stitch conversions

Note that all patterns in the book are written using US crochet terminology.
Some US terms for crochet stitches differ from the UK system. For UK conversions, please see the table below, and there is also a handy chart on the back cover flap that you can fold out for easy reference while you work. Also see the stitch glossary on pages 125–126 for an explanation of the stitches along with their abbreviations.

US term	UK term	Chart symbol
chain (ch)	chain (ch)	⌒
slip stitch (sl st)	slip stitch (sl st)	•
single crochet (sc)	double crochet (dc)	+ or ✕
half double crochet (hdc)	half treble crochet (htr)	T
double crochet (dc)	treble crochet (tr)	T
treble crochet (tr)	double treble crochet (dtr)	T
double treble crochet (dtr)	triple treble crochet (trtr)	T
double crochet 3 together (dc3tog)	treble crochet 3 together (tr3tog)	⋀
two double crochet cluster (2dccl)	two treble crochet cluster (2trcl)	⋀
three treble crochet cluster (3trcl)	three double treble crochet cluster (3dtrcl)	⋀
gauge	tension	N/A
skip	miss	N/A

Abbreviations

* **	Repeat instructions between asterisks as many times as instructed		rep	repeat
			RS	right side
cm	centimetres		sp(s)	space(s)
g	grams		st(s)	stitch(es)
in	inches		WS	wrong side
m	metres		yd	yards
NCR	new colour round		yoh	yarn over hook
RCR	repeat colour round			

Traditional granny squares

The traditional granny square is a great starting point when making clothes. The first six projects in the book use the traditional granny square so please refer to these instructions when working on those. The other projects in the book will introduce you to fun variations on the traditional granny square!

Note

The chain 3 made at the beginning of each round counts as a double crochet stitch in the traditional granny square and throughout the patterns in the book.

Round 1: 3 ch, in the ring work 2 dc, 2 ch, 3 dc, 2 ch, 3 dc, 2 ch, 3 dc, 2 ch, sl st to third of 3-ch, fasten off (you will have 4 x groups of 3 dc and 4 x 2-ch sp).

Round 2: using new colour, join yarn in any 2-ch corner space, in the same sp work (3 ch, 2 dc, 2 ch, 3 dc), 1 ch *in the next 2-ch sp work (3 dc, 2 ch, 3 dc), 1 ch**, rep from * to ** twice more, sl st to third of 3-ch, fasten off.

Tips

Always work on the right side (RS) of the granny square.

To join a new colour, put your hook through any 2-ch corner space and pull the yarn back through the space so that you have a loop on your hook. Now make one chain to fasten your new colour onto your work.

When you join your new colour, join it on the opposite corner to where you fastened off so that the square is balanced and doesn't twist.

Round 3: using new colour, join yarn in any 2-ch corner space, in same sp work (3 ch, 2 dc, 2 ch, 3 dc), 1 ch, in next 1-ch sp work 3 dc, 1 ch, *in next 2-ch sp work (3 dc, 2 ch, 3 dc), 1 ch, in next 1-ch sp work 3 dc, 1 ch**, rep from * to ** twice more, sl st to third of 3-ch, fasten off.

Round 4: using new colour, join yarn in any 2-ch sp, in same sp work (3 ch, 2 dc, 2 ch, 3 dc), 1 ch, in every 1-ch sp along edge work (3 dc, 1 ch), *in next 2-ch sp work (3 dc, 2 ch, 3 dc), 1 ch, in every 1-ch sp along edge work (3 dc, 1 ch)**, rep from * to ** twice more, sl st to third of 3-ch, fasten off.

For all further rounds repeat round 4.

Winter's Day
Scarf

This is a great project to start with if you are new to making crochet garments. It is made with chunky yarn and a 6mm (US 10, UK 4) hook so works up quickly and is super snuggly for a winter's day!

➜ Size

71¾in (182cm) long and 10¼in (26.5cm) wide

➜ Materials

Yarnsmiths Create Chunky, bulky (chunky), 100% acrylic, 3½oz/100g, 164yd/150m:

  2 balls in cornflower blue (A)

  1 ball in mustard yellow (B)

  1 ball in Christmas green (C)

  1 ball in grass green (D)

  1 ball in royal blue (E)

  1 ball in teal (F)

➜ Tools

6mm (US 10, UK 4) crochet hook

➜ Gauge (tension)

5¾in (14.5cm) at the end of round 5

➜ Pattern notes

You will make 12 granny squares, join them together and edge your scarf with the main colour. You can then add tassels for a playful finish.

1. Create your granny squares

Work the traditional granny square pattern (pages 12–13) until the end of round 5.

Work a total of 12 traditional granny squares, four in each of the three colourways in the table below.

	Round 1	Round 2	Round 3	Round 4	Round 5
Colourway 1	D	B	F	E	A
Colourway 2	E	C	D	B	A
Colourway 3	B	F	C	D	A

2. Assemble your scarf

You will now join the granny squares together in the colourway sequence, *1:2:3, rep from * three more times.

JOINING THE GRANNY SQUARES

Hold two granny squares together with RS facing. Using yarn A and working through both squares, join in any 2-ch sp, 1 ch, work 1 sc in the same 2-ch sp.

Working through consecutive sts and ch sps on both squares: *work 1 sc in each of the next 3 sts, work 1 sc in 1-ch sp**, rep from * to ** until last 3 sts, work 1 sc in each of the next 3 sts, work 1 sc in the last 2-ch sp (21 sts).

Fasten off and weave in ends.

Rep until all 12 granny squares have been joined together in the sequence described above.

3. Add the edging

Work a round of granny stripe around the edge of the scarf, as shown below.

Using yarn A and with RS facing, join in the 2-ch sp at the bottom corner of the scarf, in the same sp work (3 ch, 2 dc, 2 ch, 3 dc).

1 ch, *work (3 dc, 1 ch) in every ch sp along the side of scarf until the next corner, in the 2-ch corner sp work (3 dc, 2 ch, 3 dc), 1 ch**, rep from * to ** twice more, work (3 dc, 1 ch) in every ch sp along last side, sl st to third of 3-ch (252 sts, not including ch sps).

Fasten off and weave in ends.

4. Finish your scarf

Add tassels to the short ends of your scarf, as shown below.

ADDING THE TASSELS

Cut six 12in (30cm) lengths of yarn A. Fold all six lengths in half to make a loop, put your hook through the loop and the 2-ch sp in the corner of the short edge of your scarf.

Use your hook to grab the twelve ends of the yarn and pull them through the loop. Pull to tighten the knot.

Rep for all ch sps along the short edge (7 tassels).

Trim tassel ends with sharp scissors. Rep for the other short end of the scarf.

Winter's Day
Hat

This hat is the perfect match to your Winter's Day Scarf!

➔ Size

Finished circumference:
23½in (60cm)

Finished height: 9¾in (25cm)

➔ Materials

Yarnsmiths Create Chunky, bulky
(chunky), 100% acrylic, 3½oz/100g,
164yd/150m:

2 balls in cornflower blue (A)

1 ball in mustard yellow (B)

1 ball in Christmas green (C)

1 ball in grass green (D)

1 ball in royal blue (E)

1 ball in teal (F)

Pompom maker (to make a pompom 4in
(10cm) in diameter)

➔ Tools

6mm (US 10, UK 4) crochet hook

➔ Gauge (tension)

5¾in (14.5cm) at the end of round 5

➔ Pattern notes

You will join three granny squares
together in a loop, then gather at the top
and add an edge. The pompom finishes it
off perfectly!

If you are making a hat to match the scarf
in the previous pattern you can use the
leftover yarn, you will just need one extra
ball of yarn A.

1. Create your granny squares

Work the traditional granny square pattern on pages 12–13 until the end of round 5.

Work three granny squares – one in each of the following colourways.

	Round 1	Round 2	Round 3	Round 4	Round 5
Colourway 1	D	B	F	E	A
Colourway 2	E	C	D	B	A
Colourway 3	B	F	C	D	A

2. Join your granny squares

You will now join the three granny squares together to form a loop, as shown on the right.

Hold two granny squares together with RS facing. Using yarn A and working through both squares, join in any 2-ch sp, 1 ch, work 1 sc in the same 2-ch sp.

Working through consecutive sts and ch sps on both squares: *work 1 sc in each of the next 3 sts, work 1 sc in 1-ch sp**, rep from * to ** until the last 3 sts, work 1 sc in each of the next 3 sts, work 1 sc in the last 2-ch sp (21 sts).

Rep until all three squares are joined in a loop.

3. Assemble your hat

Thread a 12in (30cm) length of yarn A onto a tapestry needle, turn the hat inside out and thread the needle in and out of the top of the stitches all the way around the top of the hat.

Pull both ends of the yarn to gather the hat in at the top, as shown on the right. Fasten off the yarn, tying a knot to secure the gather at the top of the hat and weave in ends.

Turn the hat right side out.

4. Add the edging

BOTTOM EDGE

Round 1: using yarn A and with RS facing, join in any st at the bottom of the hat, 3 ch, work 1 dc into each st and ch sp around hat, sl st to third of 3-ch (63 sts).

Round 2: 3 ch, work 1 dc into each st around, sl st to third of 3-ch.

Round 3: rep round 2.

If you would like a deeper rib to the hat you can repeat round 2 until you have the depth required.

Weave in ends.

5. Finish your hat

Make a pompom 4in (10cm) in diameter, trim and sew it to the top of the hat.

Emily (left) is wearing the hat made in natural (A), teal (B), plum (C), lilac (D), pinkberry (E) and Christmas green (F).

Feel the Magic
Bag

This bag reminds me of my Nana's handbag – it's so spacious that it feels magical! It's the perfect place for keeping your current crochet project, and because it's made from just one granny square it's easy to make.

➔ Size

15¾ x 15¾in (40 x 40cm) (excluding handles)

➔ Materials

Drops Paris, 10-ply/worsted (aran), 100% cotton, 1¾oz/50g, 75m/82yd:
  2 balls in vanilla (A)
  2 balls in opal green (B)
  2 balls in lilac (C)
  2 balls in red (D)
  2 balls in dandelion (E)
  2 balls in recycled denim (F)
  2 balls in royal blue (G)
  2 balls in medium purple (H)
  2 balls in blush (I)
  3 balls in cream (J)
39¼in (1m) fabric to line (optional)
A pair of bamboo bag handles, 6in (15cm) in diameter

➔ Tools

5mm (US 8, UK 6) crochet hook

➔ Gauge (tension)

5in (12.5cm) at the end of round 5

➔ Pattern notes

The bag is constructed by making a large granny square. Once made, you can line the bag if you choose to. You will then decrease around the top to gather the edges together. You finish by making two tabs on the short edges to sew over the bamboo handles.

1. Work your granny square pattern

Work the traditional granny square pattern on pages 12–13 until the end of round 27. Work the rounds in the colour order *A:B:C:D:E:F:G:H:I:, rep from *.

Using yarn J, join in any 2-ch sp and work one additional round of the granny square pattern until there are 28 rounds in total (448 sts: 112 sts each side, counting each ch sp as one st).

Fasten off, weave in ends and block.

The square may seem large at this stage but don't worry, it will be smaller once assembled.

2. Assemble your bag

OPTIONAL LINING

Cut a square of fabric the same size as your bag plus a ½in (1.5cm) seam allowance all the way around.

Fold in the edges ½in (1.5cm) and press with an iron. Sew the hem in place by hand or with a sewing machine.

Sew (by hand or machine) the fabric square to your granny square with WS facing, so that the hem sits between the lining and the granny square.

SHAPE THE TOP OF THE BAG

You will now decrease to shape the top of your bag.

Move up each st marker every round as you shape the top of the bag.

Round 1: using yarn J, join in any 2-ch sp, 1 ch, work 1 sc in same 2-ch sp (place st marker in sc), *(skip 1 st, work 1 sc in the next st, skip 1 st, work 1 sc in 1-ch sp), rep 26 more times, skip 1 st, work 1 sc in the next st, skip 1 st, in next 2-ch sp work 1 sc (place st marker in sc)**, rep from * to ** three more times, on final rep sl st to first st, replace st marker, do not remove st markers (224 sts).

On round 2 you will shape the bag so that two of the sides are shorter and two are longer (see photo below).

Round 2: 1 ch, sc2tog across same st as sl st and next st *sc2tog along edge to next st marker, work (1 sc in next st, sc2tog) rep along edge to two stitches before next st marker, sc2tog across last 2 sts**, rep from * to **once more, sl st to first st (136 sts: 28 sts along short edges, 39 sts longer edges).

Round 3: 1 ch, work 1 sc in same place as sl st, work 1 sc in each st around, sl st to first st.

Rounds 4–5: rep round 3.

Fasten off and weave in ends.

Decrease along one edge at the end of round 1.

MAKE THE TABS

You will now make two tabs to attach the circular bamboo bag handles to the bag.

Using yarn J, join to a st on one of the short edges marked with a st marker.

Row 1: 1 ch, work 1 sc in same place, work 1 sc in each of next 27 sts (28 sts).

Row 2: 1 ch, turn, work 1 sc in every st along.

Rows 3–15: rep row 2.

Check the tab fits over your handles and add more repeats if necessary.

Fasten off and weave in ends.

Rep for the other short edge.

3. Finish your bag

Fold these tabs over the bamboo bag handles and sew the edges to the inside of the bag.

A Hug from Granny
Cocoon Cardigan

This beautiful cocoon style cardigan is so snuggly that it's like wearing a hug from Granny!

➜ Materials

Wendy Supreme, 8-ply/light worsted (DK), 100% acrylic, 3½oz/100g, 323yd/295m:

3(3:4:4:5:5:6:6) balls in natural (A)

1(1:1:2:2:2:3:3) ball in rose (B)

1(1:1:2:2:2:3:3) ball in raspberry (C)

1(1:1:2:2:2:3:3) ball in gold (D)

1(1:1:2:2:2:3:3) ball in eucalyptus (E)

1(1:1:2:2:2:3:3) ball in teal (F)

1(1:1:2:2:2:3:3) ball in royal (G)

➜ Tools

4mm (US 6, UK 8) crochet hook

➜ Gauge (tension)

4½in (11.5cm) at the end of round 4

➜ Pattern notes

You will make one large granny square then fold the edges in and join them to make armholes. The cardigan is then edged with a ribbing stitch.

1. Choose your size

Fit: oversized

Size	S	M	L	XL
Actual chest circumference	28–35½in (71–90cm)	35¾–39¼in (91–100cm)	39¾–43¼in (101–110cm)	43¾–47¼in (111–120cm)
Size of square Measured corner to corner	43¼in (110cm)	47¼in (120cm)	51¼in (130cm)	55in (140cm)
Depth of armhole	6¼in (16cm)	6¾in (17cm)	7½in (19cm)	8in (20cm)

Size	2XL	3XL	4XL	5XL
Actual chest circumference	48–51in (121–130cm)	51½–55in (131–140cm)	55½–59in (141–150cm)	59½–63in (151–160cm)
Size of square Measured corner to corner	59in (150cm)	63in (160cm)	67in (170cm)	70¾in (180cm)
Depth of armhole	8¼in (21cm)	8¾in (22cm)	9½in (24cm)	10¼in (26cm)

2. Create your granny squares

Work the traditional granny square pattern on pages 12–13 until it measures the size indicated in the size chart above. Work the rounds in the colour order *B:C:D:A:A:E:F:G:A:A, rep from * until the granny square is the required size.

3. Assemble your cardigan

With the RS facing up, fold the corners into the middle, as shown in the diagram opposite.

Measure from the folded edge inwards for the armhole depth, as shown in the table above, and mark with a stitch marker. Rep for the other side.

Using yarn A, join at an outside corner, working through two sides of the square, 1 ch, work 1 sc in the same place as the join, continuing to work through both sides of the square work 1 sc in every st and ch sp along to st marker, fasten off and weave in ends.

Rep for the other side and turn right side out.

CARDIGAN LAYOUT

Fold each corner to the central point and join along the lines indicated in red to create the sleeves.

Key

● Centre point

- - - Fold lines

―― Join here for sleeves

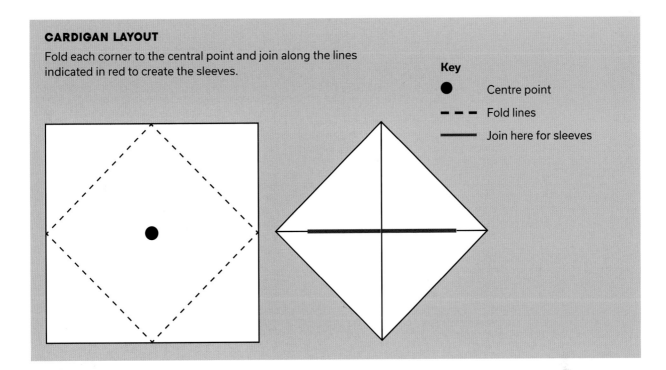

4. Add the edging

FRONT RIB

Round 1: using yarn A and with RS facing, join in bottom corner, 3 ch, work 1 dc in every st and 1-ch sp around the edge, sl st to third of 3-ch.

Round 2: 3 ch, *work 1 fpdc in next st, work 1 bpdc in following st**, rep from * to ** all the way around, sl st to third of 3-ch.

Rounds 3–10: rep round 2.

SLEEVE CUFF

Round 1: using yarn A and with RS facing, join in any st, 3 ch, work 1 dc in every st and 1-ch sp around cuff, sl st to third of 3-ch.

Round 2: 3 ch, *work 1 fpdc in next st, work 1 bpdc in following st**, rep from * to ** all the way around, sl st to third of 3-ch.

Rounds 3–10: rep round 2.

Fasten off and weave in ends.

Rep for other sleeve.

Round 2 of adding the front rib.

Tip

Always work a fpdc around a fpdc and a bpdc around a bpdc.

Memory Lane
Jacket

Everything about this jacket is nostalgic – the squares, the colours, the shape. It's the ultimate granny square garment.

➔ Materials

Wendy Supreme, 8-ply/light worsted (DK), 100% acrylic, 3½oz/100g, 323yd/295m:

3(3:4:4:5) balls in cream (A)
1(1:2:2:2) ball in pistachio (B)
1(1:2:2:2) ball in barbie pink (C)
1(1:2:2:2) ball in aster (D)
1(1:2:2:2) ball in coral (E)
1(1:2:2:2) ball in duck egg (F)
1(1:2:2:2) ball in sunshine (G)

➔ Tools

4mm (US 6, UK 8) crochet hook

➔ Gauge (tension)

Depending on the size you are making, your granny square should measure:

XS/S: 4in (10cm) to end of round 4
M/L: 5in (12.5cm) to end of round 5
XL/2XL: 6in (15cm) to end of round 6
3XL/4XL: 7in (17.5cm) to end of round 7
5XL/6XL: 8in (20cm) to end of round 8

➔ Pattern notes

The jacket is made using the join as you go technique (see page 33). You will make one complete granny square, then, for subsequent granny squares, you will join them to the previous ones as you work the final round. You will make five panels of granny squares – one for the back, two for the front panels and two for the sleeves. These panels are then joined together to make the jacket and edged with ribbing.

1. Choose your size

Fit: loose

Size	XS/S	M/L	XL/2XL	3XL/4XL	5XL/6XL
Actual chest circumference	28–35½in (71–90cm)	34¾–43¼in (91–110cm)	43¾–51¼in (111–130cm)	51½–59in (131–150cm)	59½–67in (151–170cm)
Finished chest circumference	39½in (100cm)	49¼in (125cm)	59in (150cm)	69in (175cm)	78¾in (200cm)
Finished length	21¾in (55cm)	26½in (67.5cm)	31½in (80cm)	36½in (92.5cm)	41¼in (105cm)
Sleeve length	17¾in (45cm)	19¾in (50cm)	21¾in (55cm)	22¾in (57.5cm)	25½in (65cm)

Total number of squares: 77(77:69:69:69)

For a longer length add a row of granny squares to the front and back panels, for a shorter length take a row off.

2. Work out your colour plan

Work up to round 3(4:5:6:7) then work round 4(5:6:7:8) in yarn A.

Square	Round 1	Round 2	Round 3	Round 4	Round 5	Round 6	Round 7	Round 4 (5:6:7:8)
Colourway 1: make 15 (15:13:13:13)	B	C	D	E	F	G	B	A
Colourway 2: make 17 (17:15:15:15)	E	F	G	B	C	D	E	A
Colourway 3: make 15 (15:15:15:15)	C	D	E	F	G	B	C	A
Colourway 4: make 15 (15:13:13:13)	F	G	B	C	D	E	F	A
Colourway 5: make 15 (15:13:13:13)	D	B	C	G	E	F	D	A

3. Create your first granny square

Work the traditional granny square pattern (on pages 12–13) until round 4(5:6:7:8), working last round in yarn A.

4. Create additional granny squares

JOIN AS YOU GO

For all additional granny squares you will work rounds as described for square 1, up until the end of round 3(4:5:6:7), then when you work the final round in yarn A, you will use the join as you go technique.

Joining on one side

Using yarn A join in any 2-ch sp, 3 ch, work 2 dc in the same sp, 1 ch, sl st to 2-ch sp of square 1, 1 ch, work 3 dc back in same 2-ch sp of square 2, *1 ch, sl st to the next 1-ch sp on square 1, work 3 dc in the next 1-ch sp on square 2**, rep from * to ** until you reach the next 2-ch corner sp, in the sp work (3 dc, 1 ch, sl st in the 2-ch sp of square 1, 1 ch, work 3 dc in the same 2-ch sp of square 2), now continue to work square 2 as final round instructions, with no more sl sts to square 1 so that the granny squares are only joined on one side.

Joining on two sides

Continue in the same way as for joining a square on one side – sl st in the 1-ch sps of the existing square every time you make a 1 ch on your new square. When you reach a 2-ch corner sp, sl st in the existing sl st where two squares are already joined (push your hook under two strands of the sl st).

Use the diagrams on page 34 to assemble your five panels.

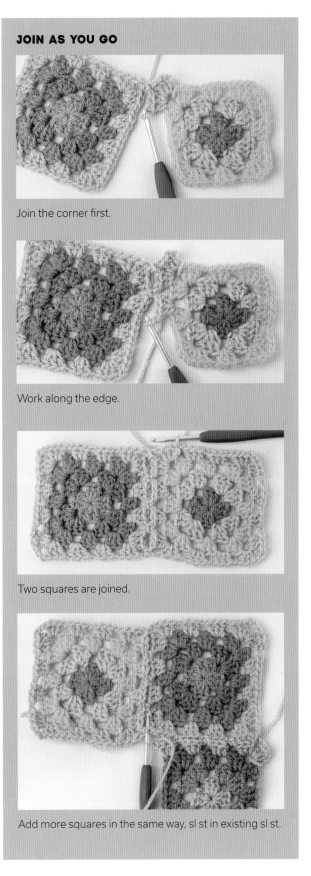

JOIN AS YOU GO

Join the corner first.

Work along the edge.

Two squares are joined.

Add more squares in the same way, sl st in existing sl st.

JACKET LAYOUT

Key

Front panels

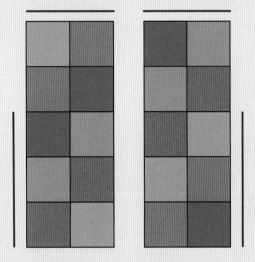

Sleeves (make 2)
Sizes XS/S:M/L

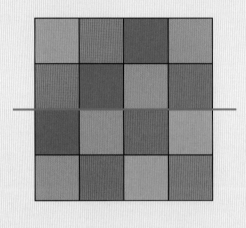

Back panel

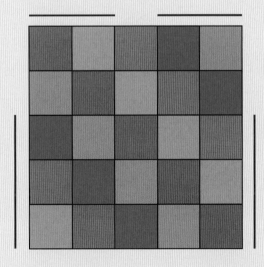

Sleeves (make 2)
Sizes XL/2XL:3XL/4XL:5XL/6XL

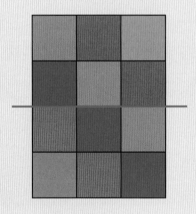

JOIN THE SHOULDER SEAMS

Place two panels with RS facing, matching the joins of the granny squares. Using yarn A and working through both panels from the outside in, join in the 2-ch sp on the top outside corner of the jacket, 1 ch, work 1 sc in same sp, work 1 sc in every st and ch sp along the shoulders for the length of two granny squares. Fasten off and weave in ends.

Rep for the other shoulder.

You will have one unworked granny square in the centre at the back. This will be the neck hole.

JOIN THE FRONT PANELS TO THE BACK ALONG THE SIDES

Working on the WS and using yarn A, join at the bottom corner working through both the front panel and the back panel, 1 ch, work 1 sc in same sp, work 1 sc in every st and ch sp along the length of three granny squares, leaving the final two squares unworked for the armhole, fasten off and weave in ends.

Rep for the other side.

ASSEMBLE THE SLEEVES

Fold the sleeve panel in half RS facing as shown by fold lines in chart. Using Yarn A and working through both sides of the panel, join at the end of a long edge, 1 ch, work 1 sc in the same sp, work 1 sc in every st and sp along, fasten off and weave in ends.

Rep for the other sleeve.

JOIN THE SLEEVES TO THE BODY

Working on the WS, match the corners of the sleeves to the armhole. Using yarn A and working through the sleeve and body, join in a 2-ch sp, 1 ch, work 1 sc in same sp, work 1 sc in every st and sp around, fasten off and weave in ends.

Rep for the other sleeve.

5. Add the edging

BOTTOM RIB

Row 1: using yarn A and with RS facing, join in the 2-ch sp at the bottom of the front panel, 3 ch, work 1 dc in every stitch and ch sp along the bottom edge of the jacket (153(189:225:261:297) sts).

Row 2: 3 ch, turn, *work 1 fpdc in next st, work 1 bpdc in following st**, rep from * to ** all the way along.

Rows 3–10: rep row 2.

Fasten off and weave in ends.

SLEEVE CUFF

Round 1: using yarn A and with RS facing, join in any st at back of sleeve, 3 ch, work 1 dc in every st and ch sp around cuff, sl st to third of 3-ch (68(84:100:116:132) sts).

Round 2: 3 ch, *work 1 fpdc in next st, work 1 bpdc in following st**, rep from * to ** until last st, work 1 fpdc, sl st to third of 3-ch.

Rounds 3–10: rep row 2.

Fasten off and weave in ends.

FRONT AND NECK EDGING

You will work all the way up one side, around the back of the neck and down the next side.

Row 1: using yarn A and with RS facing, join in 2-ch sp at bottom of front panel, 3 ch, work 1 dc in every end of row, st and ch sp up one side, around the back of the neck and down the other side (207(251:295:339:383) sts).

Row 2: 3 ch, turn, *work 1 fpdc in next st, work 1bpdc in following st**, rep from * to ** along ** all the way along.

Rows 3–10: rep row 2.

Fasten off and weave in ends.

Woodstock
Dungarees

These dungarees are wonderfully versatile – they can be worn for any occasion but would look especially fabulous at a festival!

⊖ Materials

Drops Paris, 10-ply/worsted (aran), 100% cotton, 1¾oz/50g, 82yd/75m:

13(12:13:14:15:16:17:18:19) balls in black (A)

4(5:5:6:7:8:9:10) balls in off-white (B)

3(4:4:5:6:7:8:9) balls in dandelion (C)

3(4:4:5:6:7:8:9) balls in red (D)

3(4:4:5:6:7:8:9) balls in orange (E)

3(4:4:5:6:7:8:9) balls in dark turquoise (F)

3(4:4:5:6:7:8:9) balls in opal green (G)

Set of dungaree fastenings

6 coloured beads, optional

⊖ Tools

4mm (UK 8, US 6) crochet hook

⊖ Gauge (tension)

5in (13cm) at the end of round 5

⊖ Pattern notes

The dungarees are constructed from panels of granny squares. You will start by making the panels for the tummy, then add the legs. You have the option of adding a decrease around the waist to tighten them. You will then make a separate square for the bib and finally add the back panel and straps.

1. Choose your size

Fit: loose

Size	S	M	L	XL
Actual waist measurement*	24–26¾in (61–68cm)	27¼–30in (69–76cm)	30¼–34¼in (77–87cm)	34¾–38¼in (88–97cm)
Actual hip measurement	36¼in (92cm)	39¼in (100cm)	43¼in (111cm)	48in (122cm)

Size	2XL	3XL	4XL	5XL
Actual waist measurement*	38½–42¼in (98–107cm)	42½–45¼in (108–115cm)	45¾–47¼in (116–120cm)	47¾–50in (121–127cm)
Actual hip measurement	52¾in (134cm)	56¾in (144cm)	59in (150cm)	61¾in (157cm)

*Note that there is an optional decrease for the waistline which will pull in the waist.

Select the size from the table above to calculate how many granny squares to make and how to assemble your squares into panels. It will also determine how many squares you will need for the tummy panel. Next decide which leg length to make using these inside leg measurements as a guide: short 29in (73.5cm), regular 31in (79cm), long 33in (84cm). These two measurements (tummy and leg) will give you a total number of squares.

For example, if you are making size L in regular leg length you will make 2 x 9 granny squares for the tummy panel (18), plus 5 x 5 for each of the legs (25 x 2 = 50), add these together, so 18 + 50 = 68 and this gives you the total number of squares to make. The table opposite then shows you how many to make in each colourway for your size and leg length.

Tip

When choosing which size to make, be guided by your measurement that is the largest (for me this is my waist because I am apple shaped, for pear shapes it will likely be the hips or even bottom!). So, if your waist is 33in (84cm) but your hips are 46in (117cm), make size XL. The pattern includes a drawstring waistband so that the dungarees can be tightened around the waist.

Size	Tummy panel	Legs (x 2) short (regular, long)	Total number of granny squares	Colourway 1	Colourway 2	Colourway 3	Colourway 4	Colourway 5
S	2 x 7	4 (5, 6) x 4	46 (54, 62)	10 (11, 13)	9 (11, 13)	9 (11, 12)	9 (11, 12)	9 (10, 12)
M	2 x 8	4 (5, 6) x 5	56 (66, 76)	11 (13, 15)	11 (13, 15)	11 (13, 15)	11 (13, 15)	12 (14, 16)
L	2 x 9	4 (5, 6) x 5	58 (68, 78)	11 (13, 15)	11 (13, 15)	12 (14, 16)	12 (14, 16)	12 (14, 16)
XL	2 x 10	4 (5, 6) x 6	68 (80, 92)	13 (16, 18)	13 (16, 18)	14 (16, 18)	14 (16, 19)	14 (16, 19)
2XL	2 x 11	4 (5, 6) x 6	70 (82, 94)	14 (16, 18)	14 (16, 19)	14 (16, 19)	14 (17, 19)	14 (17, 19)
3XL	2 x 12	4 (5, 6) x 7	80 (94, 108)	16 (18, 21)	16 (19, 21)	16 (19, 22)	16 (19, 22)	16 (19, 22)
4XL	2 x 13	4 (5, 6) x 7	82 (96, 110)	16 (20, 22)	16 (19, 22)	16 (19, 22)	17 (19, 22)	17 (19, 22)
5XL	2 x 14	4 (5, 6) x 8	92 (108, 124)	18 (21, 24)	18 (21, 25)	18 (22, 25)	19 (22, 25)	19 (22, 25)

2. Work out your colour plan

	Round 1	Round 2	Round 3	Round 4	Round 5
Colourway 1	B	C	D	E	A
Colourway 2	E	F	G	B	A
Colourway 3	D	B	F	G	A
Colourway 4	C	E	B	D	A
Colourway 5	F	G	B	C	A

3. Create your granny squares

Work the traditional granny square pattern until the end of round 5 in the colourways indicated in the chart on page 39, until the number of squares needed have been worked for your size.

4. Assemble your dungarees

JOIN THE GRANNY SQUARES

Hold two granny squares with RS facing and using yarn A, join in any 2-ch sp on both squares, continuing to work in consecutive sts and sps on both squares, 1 ch, work 1 sc in the same sp, work 1 sc in every st and sp along, fasten off and weave in ends.

CONSTRUCT THE PANELS

Tummy panel

Using A and working in the same way as described above, join squares into two strips of 7(8:9:10:11:12:13:14). Join the two panels together then join the two short ends together to make a loop.

Legs

Assemble the first strip of granny squares for each leg.

You will now have three loops. It works best to join the crotch before working the rest of the legs.

JOIN THE CROTCH

XS, M, XL, 3XL and 5XL sizes only:

Holding the two leg loops together and using yarn A, join two granny squares (one from each leg) in the same way as described above, all the way across the top edge of the granny square, fasten off and weave in ends (21 sts joined). Leave the rest of the squares unjoined. These will be joined to the tummy panel.

S, L, 2XL and 4XL sizes only:

Holding the two leg loops together, you will join half a granny square from each leg loop. Using yarn A, join in the 2-ch sp at the front of the trousers, 1 ch, work 1 sc in the same 2-ch sp, work 1 sc in each of the next 9 sts, fasten off and weave in ends (10 sts joined). Leave the rest of the squares unjoined. These will be joined to the tummy panel.

Join the legs for the tummy panel

Now attach the legs to the tummy panel. Turn both parts inside out and join them RS facing as described above. For sizes S, L, 2XL and 4XL, the half granny squares left from the join at the crotch will sit at the back of the dungarees.

ASSEMBLING THE CROTCH

It is useful to use stitch markers or pins to assemble the crotch before joining.

1. Join the two leg loops across a half or whole square (depending on the size you are making) for the crotch.

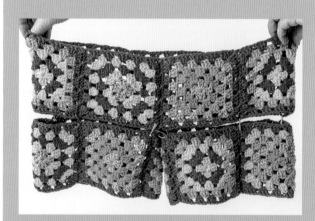

2. Join the tummy panel to the two leg loops.

MAKE THE WAISTBAND

If you would like to, you can now decrease to shape the waist. This round is optional and can be left out if you would rather not have a decrease. If possible, try the dungarees on at this stage to help you to decide!

Optional decrease round (treat each 2-ch sp and 1-ch sp as one st):

Using yarn A and with RS facing, join in any 2-ch sp at the back of tummy panel, 1 ch, work 1 sc in same 2-ch sp, sc2tog, *work 1 sc in the next st, sc2tog**, rep from * to ** all the way around, sl st to first st (98(112:126:140:154:168:182:196) sts).

If not working the decrease round (treat each of the 2-ch sp and 1-ch sp as one st):

Using yarn A and with RS facing, join in any 2-ch sp at the back of the body panel, 1 ch, work 1 sc in same 2-ch sp, work 1 sc in every st and ch sp all the way around, sl st to first st (147(168:189:210:231:252:273:294) sts).

Round 1: continuing with yarn A, 2 ch, work 1 hdc in every st all the way around, sl st to second of 2-ch.

Rounds 2–4: rep round 1.

Drawstring panel

Round 5: 2 ch, work 1 hdc in the front loop of every st around, sl st to second of 2-ch.

Round 6: 2 ch, work 1 hdc in every st around, sl st to second of 2-ch.

Round 7: 2 ch, work 1 hdc in the front loop of every st around, sl st to second of 2-ch.

Fasten off and weave in ends.

To complete the drawstring panel

Working on the inside of the dungarees, find the back loops from round 5.

Round 1: using yarn A, join in any back loop, 2 ch, work 1 hdc in the back loop of every st around in round 5, sl st to second of 2-ch (98(112:126:140:154:168:182:196) sts if decreased, 147(168:189:210:231:252:273:294) sts if no decrease worked).

Round 2: 2 ch, work 1 hdc in every st around, sl st to second of 2-ch.

Round 3: sl st in the back loop of every st in round 7.

Fasten off and weave in ends.

MAKE THE BIB

Work the traditional granny square pattern (pages 12–13) until round 9(10:11:12:13:14:15:16) in colour order *B:C:D:E:F:G:H rep from * until round 7(8:9:10:11:12:13:14) then work the final two rounds in yarn A.

From round 10 onwards you will only work three sides of the square.

Round 10: on RS, join yarn in any 2-ch space, in same sp make (3 ch, 2 dc), 1 ch, in every 1-ch sp along make (3 dc, 1 ch), *in 2-ch corner sp make (3 dc, 2 ch, 3 dc), 1 ch, in every 1-ch sp along make (3 dc, 1 ch)**, rep from * to ** once more, in final 2-ch sp make 3 dc, fasten off.

Round 11: on RS join yarn in third of 3-ch, 4 ch (counts as a st and 1-ch), make (3 dc, 1 ch) in every 1-ch sp along, *in 2-ch corner sp make (3 dc, 2 ch, 3 dc), 1 ch, make (3 dc, 1 ch) in every sp along**, rep from * to ** once more, make 1 dc in final stitch, fasten off.

Round 12: on RS join yarn in third of 4-ch, in 1-ch sp make (3 ch, 2 dc), 1 ch, make (3 dc, 1 ch) in every sp along, *in 2-ch corner sp make (3 dc, 2 ch, 3 dc), 1 ch, make (3 dc, 1 ch) in every 1-ch sp along**, rep from * to ** once more, make 2 dc in final 1-ch sp, make 1 dc in final st, fasten off.

Round 13: rep round 11.

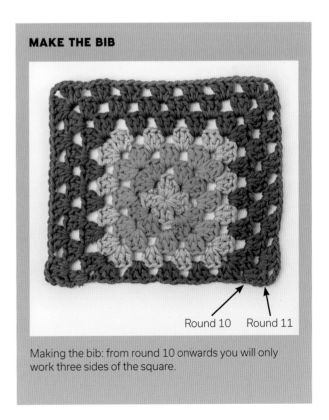

MAKE THE BIB

Round 10   Round 11

Making the bib: from round 10 onwards you will only work three sides of the square.

Round 14: rep round 12.

Round 15: rep round 11.

Round 16: rep round 12.

Fasten off and weave in ends.

Check the fit of the bib before joining. You may want to add more or fewer rounds to suit your shape.

Join the bib to the waistband

Using a st marker, mark the centre of the waistband at the front and the centre of the bib at the front. Match these up and ensure the bib is evenly positioned each side. Holding both pieces together RS facing and using yarn A, join at one end and work 1 ch, work 1 sc in the same st, work 1 sc in every st and ch sp along one side of the square, finishing with 1 sc in the last st.

Fasten off and weave in ends.

BACK PANEL

Where the waistband and front panel are joined count around 14(16:18:20:22:24:26:28) sts either side and mark the sts with a st marker. The back panel will be worked between these two st markers. Check that you are happy with this fit and adjust the position of the st markers if necessary.

Join yarn A in the first marked st.

Row 1: 2 ch, work 1 hdc in every stitch along to the next st marker.

Row 2: 2 ch, turn, work 1 hdc in every stitch along.

Rows 3–12: rep row 2.

STRAPS

Continuing straight on from the end of row 12.

Row 1: 1 ch, turn, work 1 sc in the first st and each of the next 4 sts (5 sts).

Rows 2–70: rep row 1.

Check that the strap is long enough and add more rows if necessary.

Fasten off and weave in ends.

Join yarn A on the opposite corner and rep for the second strap.

5. Finish your dungarees

MAKE THE DRAWSTRING

Make a foundation chain that is the circumference of the body plus 12in (30cm). Thread the end of the chain onto a large needle and from the front centre push through the channel of the waistband, working gradually all the way around. Bring the chain back out at the centre front one stitch before where you started. Thread three beads (one of each colour) onto each end of the drawstring and knot to secure.

ATTACH THE DUNGAREE CLIPS

Position the clips at each side of the bib and to the end of the straps.

ADD EDGING TO THE BOTTOM OF THE LEGS

Edging style 1: as modelled by Louisa on the right in the photo opppsite.

Round 1: using yarn A, on RS join in any 2-ch corner sp, 3 ch, make 1 dc in every st and ch sp around, sl st to third of 3-ch.

Round 2: 3 ch, make 1 dc in every st around, sl st to third of 3-ch.

Rep round 2 until desired length (try on for fit).

Rep for other leg.

Edging style 1: as modelled by Emily on the left in the photo opppsite.

Round 1: using yarn A, join in any 2-ch corner sp, 3 ch, make 2 dc in same sp, 1-ch, work (3 dc, 1 ch) in every ch sp around, sl st to third of 3-ch.

Round 2: sl st in next 2 sts and 1-ch sp, 3 ch, work 2 dc in same sp, work (3 dc, 1 ch) in every ch sp around, sl st to third of 3-ch.

Rep round 2 until desired length (try on for fit).

Rep for other leg.

Opposite: Louisa (right) is wearing the dungarees made in black (A), light turquoise (B), cerise (C), dandelion (D), medium pink (E), opal green (F) and lilac (G).

Note that the dungarees shown haven't included beads on the drawstring waist.

Walk in the Park
Poncho

This poncho is the perfect substitute for a jacket on a chilly day; just what you need for an autumnal stroll in the park.

➔ Materials

Scheepjes Chunky Monkey, 10-ply/ worsted (aran), 100% acrylic, 3½oz/100g, 127yd/116m:

6(7:8) balls in jasmine (A)

1(1:2) ball in teal (B)

1(1:2) ball in flame (C)

1(1:2) ball in chartreuse (D)

1(1:2) ball in deep fuschia (E)

1(1:2) ball in mustard (F)

1(1:2) ball in aqua (G)

➔ Tools

5mm (US 8, UK 6) crochet hook

➔ Gauge (tension)

S/M: 4¼in (11cm) to end of round 3

L/2XL: 5in (12.5cm) to end of round 4

3XL/5XL: 6in (15cm) to end of round 5

➔ Pattern notes

This design moves away from traditional granny squares and introduces you to the idea of a solid granny square. You will make ten granny squares for the yoke at the neck, you then add rounds of granny stripe for the body and ribbing for the cowl neck.

1. Choose your size

Fit: oversized

Size	S/M	L/2XL	3XL/5XL
Bust size	28–39¼in (71–100cm)	39¾–51¼in (101–130cm)	51½–63in (131–160cm)
Finished chest size	43¼in (110cm)	55in (140cm)	67in (170cm)

You will work a total of 3(4:5) rounds for your granny squares.

Work as stated for the relevant colourway until the end of round 2(3:4) then work the last round in yarn A.

Work a total of 10 squares – two squares in each colourway.

2. Work out your colour plan

	Round 1	Round 2	Round 3	Round 4	Final round
Colourway 1	B	C	D	E	A
Colourway 2	E	F	G	C	A
Colourway 3	D	B	E	F	A
Colourway 4	F	G	C	D	A
Colourway 5	B	E	F	G	A

3. Create a solid granny square

Make 10.

Work rounds 1 and 2 for all sizes.

4 ch, sl st to first ch to make a ring.

Round 1: 3 ch, work 2 dc in the ring, 2 ch, *work 3 dc in the ring, 2 ch**, rep from * to ** twice more, sl st to third of 3-ch, fasten off.

Round 2: join new colour in any 2-ch sp, in the same sp work (3 ch, 1 dc, 2 ch, 2 dc), make 1 dc in each of the next 3 sts *in the next 2-ch corner sp work (2 dc, 2 ch, 2 dc), work 1 dc in each of the next 3 sts**, rep from * to ** twice more, sl st to third of 3-ch, fasten off (7 sts along each edge).

GRANNY SQUARE CHART

Symbol chart for rounds 1–3 (S/M)

S/M:

Round 3: using yarn A, join in any 2-ch sp, in the same sp work (3 ch, 2 dc, 2 ch, 3 dc), 1 ch, skip 3 sts, in the next st work 3 dc, 1 ch, skip 3 sts, *in the 2-ch corner sp work (3 dc, 2 ch, 3 dc), 1 ch, skip 3 sts, in the next st work 3 dc, 1 ch, skip 3 sts**, rep from * to ** twice more, sl st to third of 3-ch, fasten off (3 x groups of 3 dc along each edge).

L/2XL:

Work rounds 1 and 2 as for S/M.

Round 3: using new colour, join in any 2-ch sp, in the same sp work (3 ch, 1 dc, 2 ch, 2 dc), work 1 dc in each of the next 7 sts, *in the next corner work (2 dc, 2 ch, 2 dc), work 1 dc in each of the next 7 sts**, rep from * to ** twice more, sl st to third of 3-ch, fasten off (11 sts along each edge).

Round 4: using yarn A, join in any 2-ch sp, in the same sp work (3 ch, 2 dc, ch 2, 3 dc), 1 ch, skip 3 sts, in the next st work 3 dc, 1 ch, skip 3 sts, in the next st work 3 dc, 1 ch, skip 3 sts, *in the next 2-ch corner sp work (3 dc, 2 ch, 3 dc), 1 ch, skip 3 sts, in the next st work 3 dc, 1 ch, skip 3 sts, in the next st work 3 dc, 1 ch, skip 3 sts**, rep from * to ** twice more, sl st to third of ch 3, fasten off (4 x groups of 3 dc along each edge).

3XL/5XL

Work rounds 1–3 as for L/2XL.

Round 4: join new colour in any 2-ch sp, in the same sp work (3 ch, 1 dc, 2 ch, 2 dc), work 1 dc in each of the next 11 sts *in the next 2-ch corner sp work (2 dc, 2 ch, 2 dc), work 1 dc in each of the next 11 sts **, rep from * to ** twice more, sl st to third of 3-ch, fasten off (15 stitches along each edge).

Round 5: using yarn A, join in any 2-ch sp, in the same sp work (3 ch, 2 dc, 2 ch, 3 dc), 1 ch, skip 3 sts, in the next st work 3 dc, 1 ch, skip 3 sts, in the next st work 3 dc, 1 ch, skip 3 sts, in the next st work 3 dc, 1 ch, skip 3 sts, *in the next 2-ch corner sp work (3 dc, 2 ch, 3 dc), 1 ch, skip 3 sts, in the next st work 3 dc, 1 ch, skip 3 sts, in the next st work 3 dc, 1 ch, skip 3 sts, in the next st work 3 dc, 1 ch, skip 3 sts**, rep from * to ** twice more, sl st to third of ch 3, fasten off (5 x groups of 3 sts along each edge).

Weave in ends and block.

Your granny square will look like this at the end of round 3 for size L/2XL.

Your granny square will look like this at the end of round 4 for size L/2XL.

4. Join the yoke

Use the diagram on the right as a guide to assemble the 10 squares.

Hold two granny squares together with RS facing. Using yarn A, join through two consecutive 2-ch corner spaces on both squares, 1 ch, work 1 sc in same space, working through consecutive sts and sps on both squares *work 1 sc in each of the next 3 sts, work 1 sc in 1-ch sp**, rep from * to ** all the way along, finishing with 1 sc in the 2-ch space, fasten off and weave in ends.

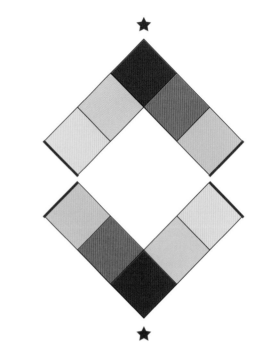

5. Shape the body

Follow colour order *A:B:A:C:A:D:A:E:A:F:A:G, rep from *.

Round 1: using yarn A and with RS facing, join in the 2-ch point at the back of the poncho (indicated by a star on the diagram), in same 2-ch sp work (3 ch, 2 dc, 2 ch, 3 dc), 1 ch, *work (3 dc, 1 ch) in every 1-ch sp along to two consecutive 2-ch corner sps, work 1 dc in the first 2-ch sp, work 2 dc in the following 2-ch sp, 1 ch**, rep from * to ** until you reach the next point at the front of the poncho (indicated by a star on the diagram), in this 2-ch sp work (3 dc, 2 ch, 3 dc), 1 ch, rep from * to ** until the end of the round, sl st to third of 3-ch, fasten off.

Round 2: using yarn B and with RS facing, join in 2-ch point at back of the poncho, in same 2-ch sp work (3 ch, 2 dc, 2 ch, 3 dc), 1 ch, work (3 dc, 1 ch) in every 1-ch sp around to next 2-ch point at the front of the poncho, in the 2-ch sp work (3 dc, 2 ch, 3 dc), 1 ch, work (3 dc, ch 1) in every 1-ch sp to the end of the round, sl st to third of 3-ch, fasten off.

Rounds 3–24: rep round 2.

6. Add the edging

DECREASE STITCHES FOR THE NECK

Round 1: using yarn A, join in 2-ch sp at base of neck on back, sc2tog across this and the next 2-ch sp, work around the edge making 1 sc in every st and 1-ch sp, when you reach two consecutive 2-ch sps, sc2tog across these two sps, sl st to first st (96(128:160) sts).

Try on and check for fit, you may not need to work the second round of decreases, in which case move straight onto round 3.

Round 2: *work 1 sc in each of the next 2 sts, sc2tog**, rep from * to ** all the way around, sl st to first st, do not fasten off (72(96:120) sts).

WORK THE NECKBAND RIB

Round 3: 3 ch, work 1 dc in every stitch around, sl st to third of 3-ch.

Round 4: 3 ch, *work 1 fpdc around the next stitch, work 1 bpdc around the following st **, rep from * to ** until last st, work 1 fpdc, sl st to third of 3-ch.

Rounds 5–22: rep round 4.

Fasten off and weave in ends.

Colour Fade
Jumper

This jumper gives you the opportunity to have a lot of fun with colour, if you choose one colour in lots of shades you can create a colour fade. The fit is inspired by vintage cricket jumpers with a wide neckband which is both flattering and makes a lovely feature.

➲ Materials

3 stitch markers

Wendy Supreme, 8-ply/light worsted (DK), 100% acrylic yarn, 3½oz/100g, 323yd/295m. Quantities are for size medium:

  1(1:1:2:2:3:3:3) ball in blush (A)
  2(2:2:3:3:3:4:4) balls in rose (B)
  3(3:4:4:4:5:5:5) balls in raspberry (C)
  4(4:5:5:5:6:6:7) balls in berry (D)

➲ Tools

4mm (US 6, UK 8) crochet hook

➲ Gauge (tension)

Depending on the size you are making, your granny square should measure (diagonal to diagonal):

S: 6¾in (17cm) to end of round 5
M: 7½in (19cm) to end of round 6
L: 8¼in (21cm) to end of round 7
XL: 9in (23cm) to end of round 8
2XL: 10in (25.5cm) to end of round 9
3XL: 10¾in (27.5cm) to end of round 10
4XL: 11½in (29cm) to end of round 11
5XL: 12¼in (31cm) to end of round 12

➲ Pattern notes

The jumper is constructed from solid granny squares which are tilted at a 90-degree angle to look like diamonds. This also creates a lovely, deep V-neck shape, for a very flattering fit. You will make two panels (one front, one back) and then work the neck onto the front panel. You will then assemble the jumper and work the sleeves onto the assembled jumper.

1. Choose your size

Fit: oversized – please note this is designed to be oversized, with an ease of 4–8in (10–20cm), please size down for a less baggy fit.

Size	S	M	L	XL
Actual chest circumference	28–35½in (71–90cm)	35¾–39¼in (91–100cm)	39¾–43¼in (101–110cm)	43¾–47¼in (111–120cm)
Finished chest circumference	40¼in (102cm)	45in (114cm)	49½in (126cm)	54¼in (138cm)
Number of rounds	5	6	7	8
Armhole depth	7in (18cm)	7½in (19cm)	8¼in (21cm)	9in (23cm)
Sleeve length (armpit to wrist)	17in (43cm)	17in (43cm)	17¼in (44cm)	17¾in (45cm)
Cropped length* (sits on or above waistline)	15¾in (40cm)	17¾in (45cm)	19¾in (50cm)	21¾in (55cm)
Medium length* (sits around hips or bottom)	20½in (52cm)	22½in (57cm)	24½in (62cm)	26½in (67cm)
Longer length* (mid-thigh)	24in (61cm)	26½in (67cm)	28¾in (73cm)	31in (79cm)

Size	2XL	3XL	4XL	5XL
Actual chest circumference	47¾–51¼in (121–130cm)	51½–55in (131–140cm)	55½–59in (141–150cm)	59½–63in (151–160cm)
Finished chest circumference	59in (150cm)	63¾in (162cm)	68½in (174cm)	73¼in (186cm)
Number of rounds	9	10	11	12
Armhole depth	9¾in (25cm)	10¾in (27cm)	11½in (29cm)	12in (30cm)
Sleeve length (armpit to wrist)	18in (46cm)	18in (46cm)	18½in (47cm)	18½in (47cm)
Cropped length* (sits on or above waistline)	23½in (60cm)	25½in (65cm)	26¾in (68cm)	27½in (70cm)
Medium length* (sits around hips or bottom)	28¼in (72cm)	30¼in (77cm)	32¼in (82cm)	34¼in (87cm)
Longer length* (mid-thigh)	33½in (85cm)	35¾in (91cm)	38¼in (97cm)	39¼in (100cm)

*Length refers to the measurement from shoulder to hem.

Work in the following order:

Round	S	M	L	XL	2XL	3XL	4XL	5XL
3	NCR Yarn B	NCR Yarn B	NCR Yarn B	NCR Yarn B	NCR Yarn B	NCR Yarn B	NCR Yarn B	NCR Yarn B
4	NCR Yarn C	NCR Yarn C	RCR	RCR	RCR	RCR	RCR	RCR
5	NCR Yarn D	RCR	NCR Yarn C	NCR Yarn C	NCR Yarn C	NCR Yarn C	RCR	RCR
6		NCR Yarn D	RCR	RCR	RCR	RCR	NCR Yarn C	NCR Yarn D
7			NCR Yarn D	NCR Yarn D	NCR Yarn D	RCR	RCR	RCR
8				RCR	RCR	NCR Yarn D	RCR	RCR
9					RCR	RCR	NCR Yarn D	NCR Yarn D
10						RCR	RCR	RCR
11							RCR	RCR
12								RCR

NCR = New colour round, RCR = Repeat colour round

CALCULATING YOUR STITCH COUNT

Round	Number of stitches along each edge (between 2-ch spaces)	Round	Number of stitches along each edge (between 2-ch spaces)	Round	Number of stitches along each edge (between 2-ch spaces)
2	7	6	23	10	39
3	11	7	27	11	43
4	15	8	31	12	47
5	19	9	35		

2. Create your granny squares

Make 15 for short, 21 for medium length, 27 for longer length.

All sizes:

Using yarn A, 4 ch, sl st to first chain to make a ring.

Round 1: 3 ch, work 2 dc in the ring, 2 ch, *work 3 dc in the ring, 2 ch**, rep from * to ** twice more, sl st to third of 3-ch, do not fasten off (4 x groups of 3 dc, 4 x 2-ch sps).

Round 2: 3 ch, work 1 dc in every st along, in the 2-ch corner work (2 dc, 2 ch, 2 dc), *work 1 dc in every st along, in the 2-ch corner work (2 dc, 2 ch, 2 dc)**, rep from * to ** twice more, sl st to third of 3-ch, fasten off.

You will now work a combination of repeat colour rounds and new colour rounds according to the chart on page 55.

New colour round (NCR): join yarn (colour specified in chart) in any 2-ch sp, in the same sp work (3 ch, 1 dc, 2 ch, 2 dc), work 1 dc in every st along, *in the 2-ch corner sp work (2 dc, 2 ch, 2 dc), work 1 dc in every st along**, rep from * to ** twice more, sl st to third of 3-ch.

Repeat colour round (RCR): 3 ch, work 1 dc in every st along to corner, *in the 2-ch corner work (2 dc, 2 ch, 2 dc), work 1 dc in every stitch along**, rep from * to ** three more times, sl st to third of 3-ch.

Fasten off when ready to start a new colour.

Tip

I have specified when to change colours as for the jumper pictured on page 53. If you would like to create your own colour order all you need to do is repeat the new colour round (NCR) for a colour change and the repeat colour round (RCR) when you want to repeat the same colour.

Round 3 worked as a new colour round.

Round 4 worked as a repeat colour round.

3. Create your granny square triangles

Make 14.

All sizes:

Using yarn A, 4 ch, sl st to first chain to make a ring.

Round 1: 5 ch, work 3 dc in the ring, 2 ch, work 3 dc in the ring, 2 ch, work 1 dc in the ring, do not fasten off (2 x groups of 3 dc, 3 x 2-ch sps).

You will now work a combination of repeat colour rounds and new colour rounds according to the chart.

Repeat colour round (RCR): 5 ch, turn, work 2 dc in the 2-ch sp, work 1 dc in every st along, in the 2-ch corner sp work (2 dc, 2 ch, 2 dc), work 1 dc in every st along, work 2 dc in the 2-ch sp, 2 ch, work 1 dc in the third of 5-ch.

New colour round (NCR): using new colour on WS, join in the first st, 5 ch, work 2 dc in the ch sp, work 1 dc in every st along, in the 2-ch corner sp work (2 dc, 2 ch, 2 dc), work 1 dc in every st along, work 2 dc in the 2-ch sp, 2 ch, work 1 dc in the third of 5-ch.

Fasten off when ready to start a new colour.

GRANNY SQUARE CHARTS

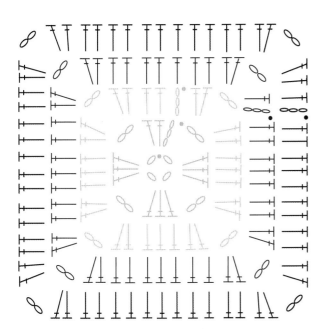

Key

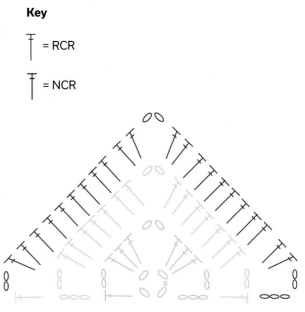

$\top$ = RCR

$\top$ = NCR

4. Create your front and back panels

Join the front and back to make two separate panels, referring to the diagrams on page 62. Hold two granny squares/triangles RS and using yarn D join through two consecutive 2-ch corner sps on both squares/triangles, 1 ch, work 1 sc in same sp, working through consecutive sts and sps on both squares/triangles work 1 sc in every st and sp along. Fasten off and weave in ends.

Turn right way out.

5. Create your neckband

You will work the neckband onto the front panel before joining the two panels together.

You will need three stitch markers.

Round 1: using yarn D, join in corner sp at top of neck edge, 1 ch, sl st in next st, work 1 sc in the next st, 1 hdc in the following st, work 1 dc in the next st, place st marker in this st, work 1 dc in every st and ch sp down to the three 2-ch spaces at the bottom of the V-neck, dc3tog across these, place st marker in this st, work 1 dc in every st and ch sp up to the last 4 sts, work 1 dc in the next st, 1 hdc in the following st, 1 sc in the next st, sl st in the last, skip the final 2-ch sp.

Round 2: 1 ch, turn, sl st in the next st, work 1 sc in the next st, 1 hdc in the following st, 1 dc in the next st, place st marker in this st, *work 1 fpdc in the next st, work 1 bpdc in the following**, rep from * to ** down to one st before st marker, dc3tog across this st, marked st and next st, rep from * to ** up to st marker, work 1 hdc in marked st, 1 sc in next st, sl st in following st.

Rounds 3–8(8:9:9:10:10:12:12): rep round 2.

SYMBOL CHART (NECKBAND)

Note: for these charts I have used a double crochet symbol instead of the front post/back post symbols. This is for the sake of clarity. Don't forget to make the fp/bp stitches when working your neckband!

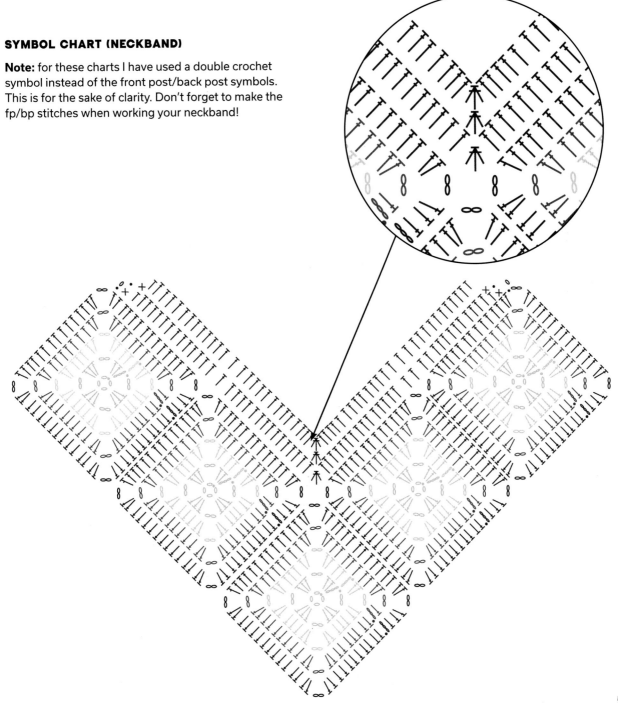

Louisa (right) is wearing the jumper made in white (A), baby blue (B), aster (C) and royal (D).

Joy-Ann (front left) is wearing the jumper made in lemon (A), sunshine (B), pumpkin (C) and cinnamon (D).

6. Assemble your jumper

Turn the jumper inside out. To join the two edges under the arm, first measure from the shoulder to the bottom of the armpit using the measurements in the size guide or your own measurements. Mark the stitch with a stitch marker – this will be your armhole. Join yarn D, in the bottom corner, 1 ch, work 1 sc in every st and ch sp, and 2 sc in the triangle end of rows up to st marker. Rep for the other side ensuring the same number of stitches are left unworked.

Now join the neckband and back panel to make the shoulders. It is useful to join this with some stitch markers, pins or large stitches first and try on to make sure that you are happy with the size of the neck. If you would like a smaller neck hole you can add more rows to the neckband. You can also gather the back panel slightly when joining to avoid it stretching. To do this skip alternate stitches on the back panel when joining to the front.

Using yarn D, join in the corner stitch. Working through both the neckband and the top of the back panel, work 1 sc in every st and ch sp across, then work 2 sc in every 2-ch sp across to next shoulder, continue to join the second shoulder to the back by working 1 sc in every st and ch sp, fasten off.

For the back of the neck (this finishes the back of the neck neatly):

Row 1: using yarn D join in st at edge of neck, 1 ch, work 1 sc in same st and every st along to opposite shoulder.

Row 2: 1 ch, turn, work 1 sc in every st along to opposite shoulder, fasten off.

You will now work the sleeves directly onto the body of the jumper.

RIGHT SLEEVE (AS WORN)

Round 1: using yarn D join in back of armhole, halfway between shoulder and arm pit, 3 ch, work 2 dc in every 2-ch sp around, sl st to third of 3-ch (count how many stitches you have and make a note so that you can ensure the second sleeve is the same).

Round 2: 3 ch, work 1 dc in every stitch around, sl st to third of 3-ch.

Rep round 2 until sleeve is 2in (5cm) less than desired length (try on or see size chart).

Rep for left sleeve.

SLEEVE CUFF

Round 1: using yarn D, join in any st, 1 ch, sc2tog all the way around, sl st to first sc.

Round 2 is optional and will depend on how tight you would like your cuff to be. If it is tight enough after round 1, skip to round 3.

Round 2: sc2tog all the way around, sl st to first sc, do not fasten off.

Round 3: 3 ch, work 1 dc in every stitch around, sl st to third of 3-ch.

Round 4: 3 ch, *work 1 fpdc in next stitch, work 1 bpdc in following stitch**, rep from * to ** all the way around, sl st to third of 3-ch.

Rounds 5–8: rep round 4.

BOTTOM EDGING

Working on right side, using yarn D join in any st on the back.

Round 1: 3 ch, work 1 dc in same place as join, work 2 dc in every end of row around, sl st to third of 3-ch.

Round 2: 3 ch, *work 1 fpdc in next stitch, work 1 bpdc in following stitch**, rep from * to ** all the way around, sl st to third of 3-ch.

Rounds 3–5: rep round 2.

JUMPER LAYOUTS, FRONT AND BACK

Key:

- - - - Fold here and join to back at stage 6 (Assemble your jumper, page 61)

SHORT LENGTH

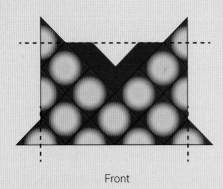

Front

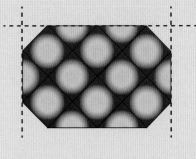

Back

MEDIUM LENGTH

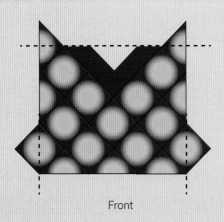

Front

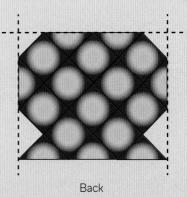

Back

LONGER LENGTH

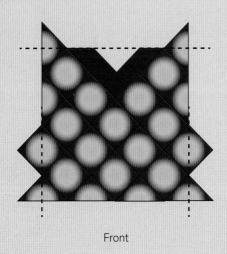

Front

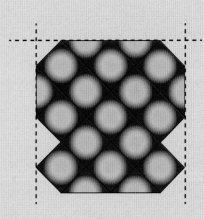

Back

Feeling Groovy
Dress

With a V-neck, adjustable waistline, loose sleeves and choice of length, this dress suits any body shape. Guaranteed to make you feel groovy!

➔ Materials

Scheepjes Catona, fingering (4-ply), 100% cotton, 1¾oz/50g, 137yd/125m. Quantities are for knee length (18 squares):

2(2:2:2:3:3:3:3) balls in lime juice (A)

2(2:3:3:3:3:4:4) balls in crystalline (B)

3(3:3:4:4:5:5:5) balls in tropic (C)

4(4:5:5:6:7:8:8) balls in jade (D)

9(9:10:10:11:11:12:12) balls in vivid blue (E)

6 coloured beads (2 of each colour), optional

➔ Tools

3mm (US 2/3, UK 11) crochet hook

➔ Gauge (tension)

Depending on the size you are making, your granny square should measure:

S: 8in (20cm) to end of round 9

M: 8½in (24cm) to end of round 10

L: 10¼in (26cm) to end of round 11

XL: 12in (30cm) to end of round 12

2XL: 12½in (32cm) to end of round 13

3XL: 13½in (34cm) to end of round 14

4XL: 14¼in (36cm) to end of round 15

5XL: 15in (38cm) to end of round 16

➔ Pattern notes

You will make large solid granny squares and two triangles, which are then joined for the bodice and sleeves. Rounds of double crochet are added for the bodice. The skirt is made from more solid granny squares which are gathered and attached at the waistline. There is an optional drawstring waist if you would like to be able to pull it in at the waist and you can adjust the length of the skirt and the body as you go along.

1. Choose your size

Fit: fitted bodice, gathered skirt

Size	S	M	L	XL
Actual chest circumference	28–35½in (71–90cm)	35¾–39¼in (91–100cm)	39¾–43¼in (101–110cm)	43¾–47¼in (111–120cm)
Finished chest circumference	31½in (80cm)	37¾in (96cm)	41in (104cm)	47¼in (120cm)
Finished length: short	29¼in (74cm)	30¾in (78cm)	32¼in (82cm)	33¾in (86cm)
Finished length: mid-length	37in (94cm)	40¼in (102cm)	42½in (108cm)	45¾in (116cm)
Finished length: long (includes 4 rows (4in/10cm) of edging)	45in (114cm)	48in (122cm)	52¾in (134cm)	57½in (146cm)

Size	2XL	3XL	4XL	5XL
Actual chest circumference	47¾–51¼in (121–130cm)	51½–55in (131–140cm)	55½–59in (141–150cm)	59½–63in (151–160cm)
Finished chest circumference	50½in (128cm)	53½in (136cm)	56¾in (144cm)	59¾in (152cm)
Finished length: short	34¾in (88cm)	36¼in (92cm)	37in (94cm)	37¾in (96cm)
Finished length: mid-length	47¼in (120cm)	49½in (126cm)	51¼in (130cm)	52¾in (134cm)
Finished length: long (includes 4 rows (4in/10cm) of edging)	59¾in (152cm)	63in (160cm)	65¼in (166cm)	67¾in (172cm)

Size	S	M	L	XL	2XL	3XL	4XL	5XL
Body length*	15¾in (40cm)	15¾in (40cm)	16½in (42cm)	16½in (42cm)	16½in (42cm)	17¼in (44cm)	17¼in (44cm)	17¼in (44cm)

*Body length is measured from shoulder to waist.

CALCULATING YOUR STITCH COUNT

Round	Number of stitches along each edge (between 2-ch sps)	Round	Number of stitches along each edge (between 2-ch sps)	Round	Number of stitches along each edge (between 2-ch sps)	Round	Number of stitches along each edge (between 2-ch sps)
2	7	6	23	10	39	14	55
3	11	7	27	11	43	15	59
4	15	8	31	12	47	16	63
5	19	9	35	13	51		

Follow the instructions in the table below, working up to round 9(10:11:12:13:14:15:16) according to your size and working repeat colour rows or new colour rows as instructed in the table. Colour changes are also shown in the table.

Round	S	M	L	XL	2XL	3XL	4XL	5XL
2	RCR	RCR	RCR	RCR	RCR	RCR	RCR	RCR
3	NCR Yarn B	NCR Yarn B	NCR Yarn B	NCR Yarn B	NCR Yarn B	NCR Yarn B	NCR Yarn B	NCR Yarn B
4	NCR Yarn C	NCR Yarn C	RCR	RCR	RCR	RCR	RCR	RCR
5	RCR	RCR	NCR Yarn C	NCR Yarn C	NCR Yarn C	NCR Yarn C	NCR Yarn C	RCR
6	NCR Yarn D	NCR Yarn D	RCR	RCR	RCR	RCR	RCR	NCR Yarn C
7	RCR	RCR	NCR Yarn D	NCR Yarn D	NCR Yarn D	RCR	RCR	RCR
8	NCR Yarn E	NCR Yarn E	RCR	RCR	RCR	NCR Yarn D	NCR Yarn D	RCR
9	RCR	RCR	NCR Yarn E	RCR	RCR	RCR	RCR	NCR Yarn D
10		RCR	RCR	NCR Yarn E	RCR	RCR	RCR	RCR
11			RCR	RCR	NCR Yarn E	RCR	RCR	RCR
12				RCR	RCR	NCR Yarn E	NCR Yarn E	NCR Yarn E
13					RCR	RCR	RCR	RCR
14						RCR	RCR	RCR
15							RCR	RCR
16								RCR

2. Create your granny squares

Make 12 for a tunic/short skirt, 18 for a mid-length skirt and 24 for a maxi length.

All sizes:

Using yarn A, 4 ch, sl st to first chain to make a ring.

Round 1: 3 ch, work 2 dc in the ring, 2 ch, *work 3 dc in the ring, 2 ch**, rep from * to ** twice more, sl st to third of 3-ch, do not fasten off (4 x groups of 3 dc, 4 x 2-ch sps).

Now follow the table according to your size to complete the square using the pattern of repeat colour rounds and new colour rounds as shown in the chart on page 67, fasten off when changing colour.

Repeat colour round (RCR): 3 ch, work 1 dc in every st along, *in the 2-ch corner sp work (2 dc, 2 ch, 2 dc), work 1 dc in every stitch along **, rep from * to ** twice more, sl st to third of 3-ch.

New colour round (NCR): using new colour, join yarn in any 2-ch sp, in the same sp work (3 ch, 1 dc, 2 ch, 2 dc), work 1 dc in every st along, *in the 2-ch corner sp work (2 dc, 2 ch, 2 dc), work 1 dc in every st along**, rep from * to ** twice more, sl st to third of 3-ch.

Follow the instructions in the table on page 67 for your size, working up to round 9(10:11:12:13:14:15:16) according to your size and working repeat colour rows or new colour rows as instructed in the table. Colour changes are also shown in the table.

3. Create your granny square triangles

Make 2.

All sizes:

Using yarn A, 4 ch, sl st to first chain to make a ring.

Round 1: 5 ch, work 3 dc in the ring, 2 ch, work 3 dc in the ring, 2 ch, work 1 dc in the ring, do not fasten off (2 x groups of 3 dc, 3 x 2-ch sps).

Now follow size guide as for squares using the table on page 67 for RCRs and NCRs.

Repeat colour round (RCR): 5 ch, turn, work 2 dc in the ch sp, work 1 dc in every st along, in the 2-ch corner sp work (2 dc, 2 ch, 2 dc), work 1 dc in every st along, work 2 dc in the ch sp, 2 ch, work 1 dc in the third of 5-ch.

New colour round (NCR): using new colour, on WS join in corner st, 5 ch, work 2 dc in the ch sp, work 1 dc in every st along, in the 2-ch corner sp work (2 dc, 2 ch, 2 dc), work 1 dc in every st along, work 2 dc in the ch sp, 2 ch, work 1 dc in the third of 5-ch.

GRANNY SQUARE CHARTS

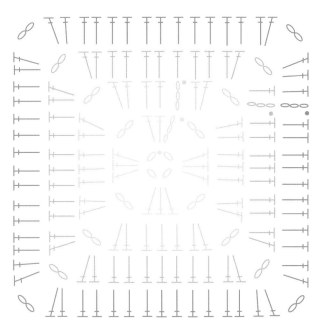

Key

$\top$ = RCR

$\top$ = NCR

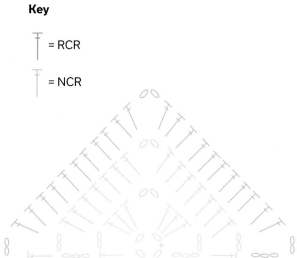

4. Assemble your dress

ASSEMBLE THE FRONT AND BACK BODICE PANELS

Using yarn E, join the front and back panels of the bodice (keeping them as two separate panels):

Holding two granny squares RS facing and using yarn E, join through two consecutive 2-ch corner sps on both squares, 1 ch, work 1 sc in the same space. Working through consecutive sts and sps on both squares, work 1 sc in every st along, finish with 1 sc in the 2-ch sp. Join the two triangles for the front panel in the bottom 2-ch sps with just one st (in the place indicated by the star in the layout diagram). Fasten off and weave in the ends.

FOR THE NECKBAND

You will now add a band to the front panel of the bodice. This is worked only on the front panel. You will then join the top of this panel to the back panel to make shoulders.

The neckband is worked in the same way as the Colour Fade Jumper, see pages 58–59.

You will need three stitch markers.

Using yarn E, join in the top corner stitch of the neckline.

Row 1: 3 ch, work 1 dc in same place as join, work 2 dc in every ch sp along to the sp before the V, dc3tog across the 3 sts at the base of the V, place st marker in this st, work 2 dc in every ch sp up to top.

Row 2: 1 ch, turn, sl st in next st, work 1 sc in the next st, work 1 hdc in the following st, 1 dc in the next st, place st marker in this st, work 1 dc in every st down to the st before the st marker at the bottom of the V-neck, dc3tog across this st, the marked st and the following st, place st marker in this st, work 1 dc in every st up to the last 4 sts, work 1 dc in the next st, work 1 hdc in the following st, 1 sc in the next st, sl st in the last st.

Row 3: 1 ch, turn, sl st in next st, work 1 sc in the next st, work 1 hdc in the following st, 1 dc in the next st, place st marker in this st, work 1 dc in every st down to the st before the st marker at the bottom of the V-neck, dc3tog across this st, the marked st and the following st, mark this st, work 1 dc in every stitch up to the st marker, make 1 hdc in this st, 1 sc in the next st, sl st in the last st.

Rows 4–6(7:8:9:10:11:12:12): rep row 2.

DRESS LAYOUT

Back bodice panel   Front bodice panel

Shorter length skirt

Knee-length skirt

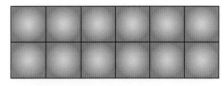

Longer length skirt

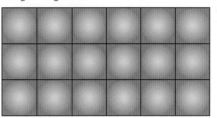

69

ASSEMBLE THE BODICE

You will now join across the top and bottom of the sleeves. Hold the two panels RS facing and using yarn E, double crochet across the top and bottom of the sleeves in the same way as you joined the squares.

Next, join the top of the neck panel to the back panel to make shoulders. Keeping the bodice inside out, join the neck and back with stitch markers, pins or basting stitches first and try on for fit.

Working through both the neck band and the top of the back panel, using yarn E, join in the corner, sl st in every stitch across (working through the neck panel and the back panel). Then sl st in every st across to the next neck edge, working 1 sl st in each 2-ch sp (this brings the back of the neck in slightly), sl st to join across the second shoulder.

Work rounds of double crochet stitches until the body length is the size indicated in the table on page 66.

For round 1, treat ch sps as a stitch.

Round 1: using yarn A with RS facing, join in any 2-ch sp at back of garment, 3 ch, work 1 dc in every st and 2-ch sp around, sl st to third of 3-ch, do not fasten off.

Round 2: 3 ch, work 1 dc in every st around, sl st to third of 3-ch, fasten off.

Round 3: using yarn B join, in same place as sl st, 3 ch, work 1 dc in every st around, sl st to third of 3-ch, do not fasten off.

Round 4: 3 ch, work 1 dc in every st around, sl st to third of 3-ch, fasten off.

Rep rounds 3 and 4 for the other colours following the order A, B, C, D, E until the body has two rounds (approximately 1in/2.5cm) to go until the desired length. You will now add a waistband.

WAISTBAND

Round 1: using yarn E with RS facing, join in any st at back of garment, 3 ch, work 1 dc in the front loop of every st around, sl st to third of 3-ch, do not fasten off.

Round 2: 3 ch, work 1 dc in the front loop of every st around, sl st to third of 3-ch, fasten off.

You will finish the waistband once you have completed the skirt.

SKIRT

Join the first row of squares as shown in the chart for the shorter skirt, single crocheting together in the same way as you did for the back body panel. Hold the two short sides RS facing and single crochet them together to make a loop. The joins will be on the inside.

Round 1: using yarn E, join in any st at the back, 1 ch, work 1 sc in the same place as join, work sc2tog across the next 2 sts, work 1 sc in the next st, *sc2tog, 1 sc**, rep from * to ** all the way around, fasten off (148(164: 180:196:212:228:244:260) sts).

Turn the skirt and body inside out and sc together, joining the decreased edge to the body, so that the join is on the inside.

Now assemble the other skirt panel(s) and join to the bottom of the skirt.

To finish the waistband:

Turn the dress inside out. Find the back loops from when you worked the waistband.

Round 1: using yarn E, join in any of the back loops, 3 ch, work 1 dc in every back loop around, sl st to third of 3-ch, do not fasten off.

Round 2: sl st to every back loop from the second round of the waistband around, fasten off.

Turn the dress right side out.

5. Finish your dress

DRAWSTRING

Make a foundation chain that is the circumference of the body + 12in (30cm). Thread the end of the chain onto a large needle and from the front centre push through the channel of the waistband, working gradually all the way around. Bring the chain back out at the centre front one stitch before where you started. Thread beads onto the chain and knot or glue to secure.

BOTTOM EDGING

Round 1: using yarn B and with RS facing, join in any 2-ch sp at back of garment, 3 ch, work 1 dc in every st and 2-ch sp around, sl st to third of 3-ch, do not fasten off.

Opposite: Louisa (right) is wearing the dress made in tulip (A), light orchid (B), amethyst (C), ultra violet (D) and petrol blue (E).

Round 2: 3 ch, work 1 dc in every st around, sl st to third of 3-ch, fasten off.

Round 3: using yarn A, join in same place as sl st, 3 ch, work 1 dc in every st around, sl st to third of 3-ch, do not fasten off.

Round 4: 3 ch, work 1 dc in every st around, sl st to third of 3-ch, fasten off.

For a longer edge you can repeat rounds 3 and 4.

SLEEVE EDGING

Round 1: using yarn B and with RS facing, join in any 2-ch sp at back of sleeve, 3 ch, work 1 dc in every st and 2-ch sp around, sl st to third of 3-ch.

Rep for other sleeve.

Fresh as a Daisy
Vest

This cotton vest is super comfortable to wear during the summer months and will keep you feeling fresh as a daisy.

➔ Materials

Cygnet 100% Cotton, 8-ply/light worsted (DK), 100% cotton, 3½oz/100g, 219yd/200m:

> 2(2:3:3:3:4:4:4:4) balls of vanilla cream (A)
>
> 1(1:1:1:2:2:2:3:3) ball of golden (B)
>
> 1(1:1:1:2:2:2:3:3) ball of white (C)
>
> 2(2:3:3:3:4:4:4:4) balls of spring (D)

➔ Tools

4mm (US 6, UK 8) crochet hook

➔ Gauge (tension)

4in (10cm) at the end of round 4

➔ Pattern notes

The daisy vest introduces you to a circle inside a granny square. You will start with a circle (the daisy shape) and then turn it into a square! The vest is then constructed from daisy squares. You will join the squares together into one large panel (to form the front and back in one piece) and join the short ends of the panel into a tube, then add straps. You can choose to make narrow or wider straps. You can also add additional squares at the bottom of the panel for a longer vest.

Opposite: Louisa (left) is wearing the vest made in white (A and C), golden (B) and lagoon (D).

1. Choose your size

Fit: fitted

Consider the fit you would like when choosing a size to make – for a tight fit, size down to allow for negative ease. For a looser fit, size up. For example, if your chest circumference is 45¼in (115cm) make the size L for a tight fit or XL for a looser fit.

Size	XS	S	M	L	XL
Actual chest circumference	28–31½in (71–80cm)	32–35½in (81–90cm)	35¾–39¼in (91–100cm)	39¾–43¼in (101–110cm)	43¾–47¼in (111–120cm)
Finished chest circumference	31in (80cm)	35in (90cm)	39in (100cm)	43in (110cm)	47in (120cm)

Size	2XL	3XL	4XL	5XL
Actual chest circumference	47¾–51¼in (121–130cm)	52–55in (131–140cm)	55½–59in (141–150cm)	59½–63in (151–160cm)
Finished chest circumference	51¼in (130cm)	55in (140cm)	59in (150cm)	63in (160cm)

Work a total of 24(27:30:33:36:39:42:45:48) daisy squares in the following layout:

Size	XS	S	M	L	XL	2XL	3XL	4XL	5XL
Number of daisy squares (depth x width)	3 x 8	3 x 9	3 x 10	3 x 11	3 x 12	3 x 13	3 x 14	3 x 15	3 x 16

2. Create a daisy granny square

Make the number of squares indicated in the size guide.

Always work on the right side.

Using yarn B, 4 ch, sl st to first ch to make a ring.

Round 1: 3 ch, work 11 dc in the ring, sl st, to third of 3-ch, fasten off (12 sts).

Round 2: using yarn C, join in any st, in same place work (3 ch, 1 dc), 1 ch, *work 2 dc in next st, 1 ch**, rep from * to ** all the way around, sl st to third of 3-ch, fasten off (12 x groups of 2 dc, 12 x 1-ch sps).

You will now shape the circle into a square.

Round 3: using yarn D, join in any 1-ch sp, in same 1-ch sp work (4 ch, 2 tr, 2 ch, 3 tr), work 3 dc in each of the next two 1-ch sps, *in the following 1-ch sp work (3 tr, 2 ch, 3 tr), work 3 dc in each of the next two 1-ch sps**, rep from * to ** twice more, sl st to fourth of 4-ch, fasten off (12 sts along each edge).

For round 4 you will work in the gap between groups of 3 sts.

Round 4: using yarn A, join in any 2-ch corner sp, in same sp make (3 ch, 2 dc, 2 ch, 3 dc), work 3 dc in every gap along, *in next 2-ch corner sp work (3 dc, 2 ch, 3 dc), work 3 dc in every gap along**, rep from * to ** twice more, sl st to third of 3-ch, fasten off (15 sts along each edge).

Weave in ends and block.

DAISY GRANNY SQUARE CHART

3. Assemble your vest

JOIN THE DAISY SQUARES

Hold two daisy squares together with RS facing and using yarn A, join through two consecutive 2-ch corner spaces on both squares, 1 ch, make 1 sc in the same space. Working through consecutive sts and sps on both squares, make 1 sc in every stitch along, finishing with 1 sc in the 2-ch space, fasten off and weave in ends.

Working in the same way, join your squares into three strips as specified in the size chart, then join these strips together.

Now hold the two short ends RS facing and join in the same way to make a loop.

4. Add the edging

You will edge around the top and bottom of the vest in single crochet stitches.

TOP EDGING

Round 1: using yarn A and with RS facing, join in any 2-ch sp, 1 ch, work 1 sc in same sp, work 1 sc in every st and 2-ch sp around top of vest, sl st to first st (136(153: 170:187:204:221:238:255:272) sts).

Round 2: 1 ch, work 1 sc in same st, work 1 sc in every st around, sl st to first st.

Round 3: rep round 2, fasten off and weave in ends.

BOTTOM EDGING

Round 1: using yarn A and with RS facing, join in any 2-ch corner sp, 1 ch, work 1 sc in sp, work 1 sc in every st and 2-ch sp around bottom of vest, sl st to first st, fasten off and weave in ends (136(153:170:187:204:221:238:255: 272) sts).

5. Make the straps

You can choose between narrow (pictured) or wide straps. I have included strap measurements but, if possible, it is best to measure for fit before assembly.

NARROW STRAP (MAKE 2)

Using yarn A, 6 ch.

Row 1: work 1 sc in the second ch from hook, work 1 sc in every ch to end (5 sts).

Row 2: 1 ch, turn, work 1 sc in every st to end.

Rep row 2 until strap measures 9½(10¼:11½:12¼: 13½:14½:15¼:16½:17¾)in/24(26:29:31:34:37:39: 42:45)cm.

Check the fit of the strap and make the strap longer or shorter if necessary.

WIDE STRAP (MAKE 2)

Using yarn A, 11 ch.

Row 1: work 1 sc in the second ch from hook, work 1 sc in every ch to end (10 sts).

Row 2: 1 ch, turn, work 1 sc in every st to end.

Rep row 2 until strap measures 9½(10¼:11½:12¼: 13½:14½:15¼:16½:17¾)in 24(26:29:31:34:37:39: 42:45)cm.

Check the fit of the strap and make the strap longer or shorter if necessary.

JOIN THE STRAPS TO THE BODY

Check the positioning of your straps before sewing them on. I used the position of bra straps as a guide as to where to sew them.

Sew straps to the body panel of daisy squares approximately 3½in (9cm) from under arm on both front and back.

Fresh as a Daisy
Shorts

These shorts look super cute on their own or paired with the Fresh as a Daisy Vest.

◑ Materials

Cygnet 100% Cotton, 8-ply/light worsted (DK), 100% cotton, 3½oz/100g, 219yd/200m:

2(2:3:3:3:4:4:4:4) balls of vanilla cream (A)

1(1:1:1:2:2:2:3:3) ball of golden (B)

1(1:1:1:2:2:2:3:3) balls of white (C)

2(2:3:3:3:4:4:4:4) balls of spring (D)

6 beads of your choice

◑ Tools

4mm (US 6, UK 8) crochet hook

◑ Gauge (tension)

4in (10cm) at the end of round 4

◑ Pattern notes

The shorts are constructed by making the same daisy squares as used for the vest. You will join the squares together into three panels then join the panels into tubes (to form the waist and two legs). You will then add a drawstring waistband. You can add more panels to make the legs longer if you would like to.

1. Choose your size

Fit: fitted, size up for a looser fit.

Size	XS	S	M	L	XL
Waist	23½in (60cm)	24–26¾in (61–68cm)	27¼–30in (69–76cm)	30¼–34¼in (77–87cm)	34–38in (88–97cm)
Hips	33¾in (86cm)	36¼in (92cm)	39¼in (100cm)	43¾in (111cm)	48in (122cm)

Size	2XL	3XL	4XL	5XL
Waist	38½–42in (98–107cm)	42½–45¼in (108–115cm)	45¾–47¼in (116–120cm)	47¾–50in (121–127cm)
Hips	52¾in (134cm)	56¾in (144cm)	59in (150cm)	61¾in (157cm)

Body: work a total of 16(18:20:22:24:26:28:30:32) daisy squares for the body in the following layout.

Size	XS	S	M	L	XL	2XL	3XL	4XL	5XL
Number of daisy squares (depth x width)	2 x 8	2 x 9	2 x 10	2 x 11	2 x 12	2 x 13	2 x 14	2 x 15	2 x 16

Legs: work a total of 5(5:6:6:7:7:8:8:9) daisy squares for each leg in the following layout.

Size	XS	S	M	L	XL	2XL	3XL	4XL	5XL
Number of daisy squares (x 2) (depth x width)	1 x 5	1 x 5	1 x 6	1 x 6	1 x 7	1 x 7	1 x 8	1 x 8	1 x 9

Tip

When choosing which size to make, be guided by your measurement (waist, hips or bottom) that is the largest (for me this is my waist because I am apple shaped, for pear shapes it is likely to be the hips or bottom). So, if your waist is 34in (86.5cm) but your hips are 44in (112cm), make size XL. The waistband is drawstring so is adjustable.

2. Create your daisy granny squares

Follow the instructions for Fresh as a Daisy Vest to make 26(28:32:34:38:40:44:46:50) daisy squares (page 75).

3. Assemble your shorts

JOIN THE GRANNY SQUARES

Hold two daisy squares together with RS facing and using yarn A, join through two consecutive 2-ch corner spaces on both squares, 1 ch, work 1 sc in the same sp, working through consecutive sts and sps on both squares work 1 sc in every st along, finishing with 1 sc in the 2-ch space, fasten off and weave in ends.

CONSTRUCT THE PANELS

Join your squares into strips then join these strips together into panels as specified for the body and two legs.

BODY

For each panel, hold the two short ends RS facing and join to make a loop.

You will now have three loops.

For photographs of the joining technique, see page 33.

EXAMPLE PANEL LAYOUT FOR SIZE L

Key

—— Join body panel here

—— Join each leg panel here

—— Join here for the crotch

Body panel

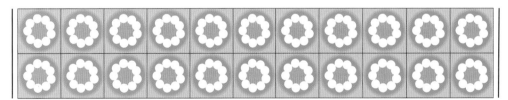

Legs

JOIN AT THE CROTCH

XS, M, XL, 3XL and 5XL sizes only:

Hold the two leg loops together with RS facing and using yarn A, you will join two granny squares (one from each leg) all the way across one edge. Join yarn A in the 2-ch sp at the front of the shorts, 1 ch, work 1 sc in same place, work 1 sc in each of the next 16 sts, fasten off, leaving the rest of the squares unjoined, these will be joined to the body panel (17 sts).

S, L, 2XL and 4XL sizes only:

Hold the two leg loops together with RS facing and using yarn A, you will join half a granny square from each leg loop. Join yarn A in the 2-ch sp at the front of the shorts, 1 ch, work 1 sc in same place, work 1 sc in each of the next 8 sts, fasten off, leaving the rest of the squares unjoined – these will be joined to the body panel (9 sts).

JOIN THE LEGS TO THE BODY

Turn both parts inside out and join them RS facing using yarn A. Then turn right sides out. For size S, L, 2XL, 4XL, the half granny squares left from the join at the crotch will sit at the back of the shorts.

4. Add the edging

You will edge around the top and bottom of the shorts in single crochet stitches.

BOTTOM LEG EDGING

Round 1: using yarn A and with RS facing, join in any 2-ch sp on the bottom of one leg, 1 ch, work 1 sc in same 2-ch sp, work 1 sc in every st and 2-ch sp around bottom of leg, sl st to first st, fasten off and weave in ends (85(85:102:102:119:119:136:136:153) sts).

Rep for the second leg.

TOP EDGING

Round 1: using yarn A and with RS facing, join in any 2-ch sp, 1 ch, work 1 sc in same 2-ch sp, work 1 sc in every st and 2-ch sp around top of shorts, sl st to first st (136(153:170:187:204:221:238:255:272) sts).

Round 2: 1 ch, work 1 sc in same place, work 1 sc in every st around, sl st to first st.

Rounds 3 and 4: rep round 2.

For round 5 you will work in the front loops only for all sts.

Round 5: 1 ch, work 1 front loop sc in same place, work 1 front loop sc in every st around, sl st to first st.

Now continue working into both loops of the stitch.

Rounds 6–10: rep round 2.

Fold the waistband in half inwards. Using yarn A, work 1 sl st into each back loop remaining from working round 5 to make a channel, fasten off and weave in ends.

5. Finish your shorts

Make a chain that is your waist circumference plus 12in (30cm).

Thread the chain onto a tapestry needle and find the centre front of the waistband. Now count 2 sts to the left and thread the tapestry needle through a gap between sts into the channel you made. Push the needle through the channel all the way around the waistband and bring out 4 sts before the place you started.

Thread one bead of each colour onto each end of the chain and tie a knot underneath the beads to secure them.

Feel the Sunshine
Shrug

This beautiful circle in a square design looks like rays of sunshine and the lightweight yarn makes the shrug a perfect summer cover up – beautiful over a dress or T-shirt!

➔ Materials

Drops Alpaca, Sport (5-ply), 100% alpaca, 1¾oz/50g, 183yd/167m:

- 4(4:5:5:6) balls in dark turquoise (A)
- 1(1:1:1:1) ball in goldenrod (B)
- 2(2:2:2:2) balls in orange (C)
- 2(2:2:2:2) balls in light blue (D)

4 beads in two colours, optional

➔ Tools

3mm (US 2/3, UK 11) crochet hook

➔ Gauge (tension)

Depending on the size you are making, your granny square should measure:

XS/S: 4in (10cm) to end of round 4

M/L: 4¾in (12cm) to end of round 5

XL/2XL: 5½in (14cm) to end of round 6

3XL/4XL: 6¼in (16cm) to end of round 6

5XL/6XL: 7in (18cm) to end of round 7

➔ Pattern notes

The shrug is worked with a sport (5-ply) alpaca yarn. You will make sunray granny squares and triangles which are joined into three panels to be assembled into the shrug. There is a tie at the V-neck to secure it.

1. Choose your size

Fit: loose

Size	XS/S	M/L	XL/2XL	3XL/4XL	5XL/6XL
Actual chest circumference	28–35½in (71–90cm)	35¾–43¼in (91–110cm)	43¾–51¼in (111–130cm)	51½–59in (131–150cm)	59½–67in (151–170cm)
Finished chest circumference	39¼in (100cm)	47½in (120cm)	55in (140cm)	63in (160cm)	71in (180cm)
Finished length	13¾in (35cm)	16¼in (41cm)	18½in (47cm)	20¾in (53cm)	23¼in (59cm)
Finished sleeve length	8in (20cm)	9½in (24cm)	11in (28cm)	12½in (32cm)	14¼in (36cm)

Louisa is wearing the shrug made in lime (A), goldenrod (B), light pink (C) and dark pink (D).

2. Create your sunray granny squares

Make 33.

All sizes:

Using yarn B, 4 ch, sl st to first ch to make a ring.

Round 1

Round 2

Round 1: ch 4 (counts as a st and 1-ch sp), *in the ring work 1 dc, 1 ch**, rep from * to ** ten more times, sl st to third of 4-ch, fasten off (12 x dc, 12 x 1-ch).

Round 2: using yarn C, join in any 1-ch sp, in same sp work (4 ch, 1 tr), 1 ch, *in next ch sp work 2 tr, 1 ch**, rep from * to ** all the way around, sl st to fourth of 4-ch, fasten off (12 x 2 tr, 12 x 1-ch).

Round 3: using yarn D, join in any 1-ch sp, in same sp work (4 ch, 2 tr), 2 ch, *in next ch sp work 3 tr, 2 ch**, rep from * to ** all the way around, sl st to fourth of 4-ch, fasten off (12 x 3 tr, 12 x 2-ch).

Round 3

You will now shape the circle into a square.

Round 4: using yarn A, join in any 2-ch sp, in same sp work (5 ch, 2 dtr, 4 ch, 3 dtr), *ch 3, in next 2-ch sp work 3 tr, 3 ch, in next 2-ch sp work 3 tr, 3 ch, in next 2-ch sp work (3 dtr, 4 ch, 3 dtr)**, rep from * to ** twice more, 3 ch, in next 2-ch sp work 3 tr, 3 ch, in next 2-ch sp work 3 tr, 3 ch, sl st to fifth of 5-ch.

S/M size only: fasten off.

SUNRAY GRANNY SQUARE CHART (ROUNDS 1-4)

M/L:

Round 5: sl st in each of next 2 sts, sl st in 4-ch sp, in same sp make (4 ch, 2 tr, 4 ch, 3 tr), *3 ch, work (3 dc, 3 ch) in every sp along to next 4-ch corner sp, in corner make (3 tr, 4 ch, 3 tr)**, rep from * to ** twice more, 3 ch, make (3 dc, 3 ch) in every sp along to next corner, sl st to fourth of 4-ch.

Fasten off.

XL/2XL:

Round 5: sl st in each of next 2 sts, sl st in 4-ch sp, in same sp work (5 ch, 2 dtr, 4 ch, 3 dtr), *3 ch, (3 tr, 3 ch) in every sp along to next 4-ch corner sp, in corner work (3 dtr, 4 ch, 3 dtr)**, rep from * to ** twice more, 3 ch, work (3 tr, 3 ch) in every sp along to final corner, sl st to fifth of 5-ch.

Round 6: sl st in each of next 2 sts, sl st in 4-ch sp, in same sp make (4 ch, 2 tr, 4 ch, 3 tr), *3 ch, work (3 dc, 3 ch) in every sp along to next corner 4-ch sp, in corner work (3 tr, 4 ch, 3 tr)**, rep from * to ** twice more, 3 ch, work (3 dc, 3 ch) in every sp along to next corner, sl st to fourth of 4-ch.

Fasten off.

3XL/4XL:

Round 5: sl st in each of next 2 sts, sl st in 4-ch sp, in same sp work (5 ch, 2 dtr, 4 ch, 3 dtr), *3 ch, work (3 tr, 3 ch) in every sp along to next corner 4-ch sp, in corner work (3 dtr, 4 ch, 3 dtr)**, rep from * to ** twice more, 3 ch, work (3 tr, 3 ch) in every sp along to next corner, sl st to fifth of 5-ch.

Round 6: Rep round 5.

Fasten off.

5XL/6XL:

Work up to round 6 as for 3XL/4XL.

Round 7: sl st in each of next two sts, sl st in 4-ch sp, in same sp work (4 ch, 2 tr, 4 ch, 3 tr), *3 ch, work (3 dc, 3 ch) in every sp along to next corner 4-ch sp, in corner work (3 tr, 3 ch, 3 tr)**, rep from * to ** twice more, 3 ch, work (3 dc, 3 ch) in every sp along to next corner, sl st to fourth of 4-ch.

Fasten off.

3. Create your sunray granny square triangles

Make two.

All sizes

Using yarn B, 4 ch, sl st to first ch to make a ring.

Row 1: 4 ch (counts as a st and 1-ch sp), *in the ring work 1 dc, 1 ch**, rep from * to ** three more times, work 1 dc in the ring, fasten off (6 x dc, 5 x 1-ch sp).

Row 2: using yarn C with RS facing, join in third of 4-ch at start of row 1, ch 5 (counts as a st and 1-ch sp), in next 1-ch sp (made by the fourth of 4-ch) work 2 tr, 1 ch, *in next 1-ch sp work 2 tr, 1 ch**, rep from * to ** three more times, 1 ch, work 1 tr in final st, fasten off (5 x 2 tr, 6 x 1-ch sp).

Row 3: using yarn D with RS facing join in fourth of 5-ch, 6 ch (counts as a st and 2-ch sp), in 1-ch sp made by fifth ch work 3 tr, 2 ch, *in next 1-ch sp work 3 tr, 2 ch**, rep from * to ** four more times, 2 ch, work 1 tr in final st, fasten off (6 x 3 tr, 7 x 2-ch sp).

Row 4: using yarn A with RS facing, join in the fourth of 6-ch, 7 ch (counts as a st and 2-ch sp), in 2-ch sp made by fifth and sixth ch, work 3 dtr, 3 ch, in next 2-ch sp work 3 tr, 3 ch, in next 2-ch sp work 3 tr, 3 ch, in next 2-ch sp work (3 dtr, 4 ch, 3 dtr), 3 ch, in next 2-ch sp work 3 tr, 3 ch, in next 2-ch sp work 3 tr, 3 ch, in final sp work 3 dtr, 2 ch, work 1 dtr in final stitch do not fasten off.

S size only: fasten off.

Row 1

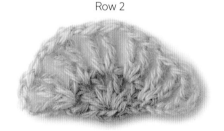

Row 2

Row 3

Row 4

M/L:

Row 5: 6 ch (counts as a st and 2-ch sp), turn, in the first 2-ch sp work 3 tr, 3 ch, work (3 dc, 3 ch) in every sp along, in the 4-ch corner sp, work (3 tr, 4 ch, 3 tr), 3 ch, work (3 dc, 3 ch) in every sp along to 7-ch, in fifth of 7-ch work (3 tr, 2 ch, 1 tr).

Fasten off.

XL/2XL:

Row 5: 7 ch (counts as st and 2-ch sp), turn, in the first 2-ch sp work 3 dtr, 3 ch, work (3 tr, 3 ch) in every sp along, in the 4-ch corner sp, work (3 dtr, 4 ch, 3 dtr), 3 ch, work (3 tr, 3 ch) in every sp along to 6-ch, in fourth of 6-ch work (3 dtr, 2 ch, 1 dtr).

Row 6: 6 ch (counts as a st and 2-ch sp), turn, in the first 2-ch sp work 3 tr, 3 ch, work (3 dc, 3 ch) in every sp along in the 4-ch corner sp, work (3 tr, 4 ch, 3 tr), 3 ch, work (3 dc, 3 ch) in every sp along to 7-ch, in fifth of 7-ch work (3 tr, 2 ch, 1 tr).

Fasten off.

3XL/4XL:

Row 5: 7 ch (counts as st and 2-ch sp), turn, in the first 2-ch sp work 3 dtr, 3 ch, work (3 tr, 3 ch) in every sp along, in the 4-ch corner sp, work (3 dtr, 4 ch, 3 dtr), 3 ch, work (3 tr, 3 ch) in every sp along to 6-ch, in fourth of 6-ch work (3 dtr, 2 ch, 1 dtr).

Row 6: rep round 5.

Fasten off.

5XL/6XL:

Work up to round 6 as for 3XL/4XL.

Row 7: 6 ch (counts as a st and 2-ch sp), turn, in the first 2-ch sp work 3 tr, 3 ch, work (3 dc, 3 ch) in every sp along, in the 4-ch corner sp, work (3 tr, 4 ch, 3 tr), 3 ch, work (3 dc, 3 ch) in every sp along to 7-ch, in fifth of 7-ch work (3 tr, 2 ch, 1 tr).

Fasten off.

**SUNRAY GRANNY SQUARE
TRIANGLE CHART (ROUNDS 1-4)**

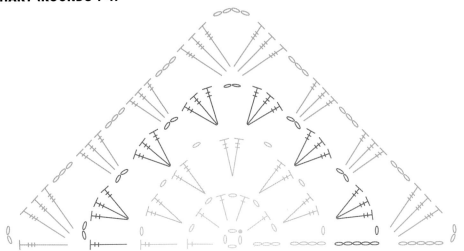

4. Assemble your shrug

Hold two squares RS facing. Using yarn A, join through two consecutive 4-ch corner sps on both squares, 1 ch, work 2 sc in the same sp, working through consecutive sts and sps on both squares work 1 sc in every st along, and 2 sc in every ch sp along, finishing with 2 sc in the 4-ch sp. Fasten off and weave in ends.

Join into strips first and then panels using the diagrams below as a guide.

Place the two front panels on top of the back panel with RS together, matching the seams of the squares. Using yarn A, join in the 4-ch sp on the outside corner, working through consecutive sts and sps, work 1 sc in every stitch and 2 sc in every ch along the shoulder seam for the length of two squares, fasten off and weave in ends.

Rep for the right shoulder seam.

Rep for underarms and bottom of sleeves.

Three squares in the centre of the back and the two half squares on the front will remain unworked for the neck.

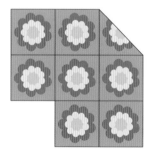
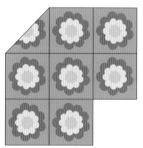

Front

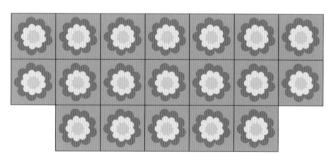

Back

5. Add the edging

BOTTOM EDGING

Row 1: using yarn A, and with RS facing, join in the 4-ch sp at the bottom edge at the front, 1 ch, work 2 sc in same 4-ch sp, work 1 sc in every st and 2 sc in every ch sp around bottom of shrug.

Row 2: 1 ch, turn, work 1 sc in every st around.

Fasten off and weave in ends.

FRONT EDGING

Using yarn A and with RS facing, join in the 4-ch sp at the bottom edge, 3 ch, work 1 dc in every st and 2 dc in every ch sp up the front edge. When you reach the bottom corner of the first triangle make (1 dc, 1 ch, 1 dc) in that corner, st mark the 1-ch sp just worked, work 2 dc in every end of row along the triangle, work 1 dc in every st and 2 dc in every ch sp along the back of the neck, work 2 dc in every end of row along the triangle, when you reach the bottom corner of the triangle work (1 dc, 1 ch, 1 dc) in that corner, mark the 1-ch sp just worked, continue to work 1 dc in every st and 2 dc in every ch sp to bottom of shrug.

Row 2: 3 ch, turn, work 1 dc in every st around, when you reach st marker make (1 dc, 1 ch, 1 dc) in the sp, mark the 1-ch sp.

Row 3: rep row 2.

Fasten off and weave in ends.

SLEEVE EDGING

Using yarn A and with RS facing, join in any st at the back of the sleeve, 1 ch, work 1 sc in same st, work 1 sc in every st around, sl st to first sc.

Fasten off and weave in ends.

5. Finish your shrug

TIE (MAKE 2)

Using yarn A, work 61 ch.

Row 1: sl st in second ch from hook, work 1 sl st in every ch (60 sts).

Using yarn A, sew one tie to each 1-ch sp at bottom of triangles on front panel (marked by st marker).

Thread one bead of each colour onto each end of the chain and tie a knot underneath the beads to secure them.

Carefree
Coatigan

This longer length hooded jacket looks fabulous on. It is made from a lightweight cotton that is super comfy to wear. The hood gives you added warmth on a chilly day, making it the perfect coatigan.

➔ Materials

Scheepjes Softfun, 8-ply/light worsted (DK), 60% cotton/40% acrylic, 1¾oz/50g, 153yd/140m:

10(12:14:16:18) balls in lagoon (A)

3(3:4:4:5) balls in salmon (B)

3(3:4:5:6) balls in peacock (C)

3(4:5:6:7) balls in lichen (D)

2(3:4:5:6) balls in jam (E)

2(3:4:5:6) balls in rose (F)

2(3:4:5:6) balls in bright turquoise (G)

4 toggle buttons, optional

➔ Tools

4mm (US 6, UK 8) crochet hook

➔ Gauge (tension)

Depending on the size you are making, your granny square should measure:

XS/S: 4in (10cm) to end of round 5

M/L: 4¾in (12cm) to end of round 6

XL/2XL: 5½in (14cm) to end of round 7

3XL/4XL: 6¼in (16cm) to end of round 8

5XL/6XL: 7in (18cm) to end of round 9

➔ Pattern notes

Made from fun circles within granny squares. You will make six panels – two for the front, one for the back, two for the sleeves and one for the hood. The coatigan is then assembled and finished off with ribbing. The cuffs are decreased to bring them in.

1. Choose your size

Fit: loose

Size	XS/S	M/L	XL/2XL	3XL/4XL	5XL/6XL
Actual chest circumference	28–35½in (71–90cm)	35¾–43¼in (91–110cm)	43¾–51¼in (111–130cm)	51½–59in (131–150cm)	59½–67in (151–170cm)
Finished chest circumference	39¼in (100cm)	47¼in (120cm)	55in (140cm)	63in (160cm)	70¾in (180cm)
Finished length	25½in (65cm)	30¾in (78cm)	34¾in (88cm)	39¼in (100cm)	44in (112cm)
Sleeve length	16¼in (41cm)	17¾in (45cm)	18½in (47cm)	20¾in (53cm)	22½in (57cm)
Number of rounds worked	5	6	7	8	9

Emily is wearing the coatigan made in peach (A), kelly (B), violet (C), canary (D), pumpkin (E), cerise (F) and dark turquoise (G).

2. Work out your colour plan

Colourway	Round 1	Round 2	Round 3	Round 4
Colourway 1: make 19(17:17:17)	C	D	E	F
Colourway 2: make 20(18:18:18)	E	G	B	D
Colourway 3: make 22(20:20:20)	F	D	C	G
Colourway 4: make 20(20:20:20)	D	F	G	B
Colourway 5: make 20(18:18:18)	B	C	D	E

COATIGAN LAYOUTS

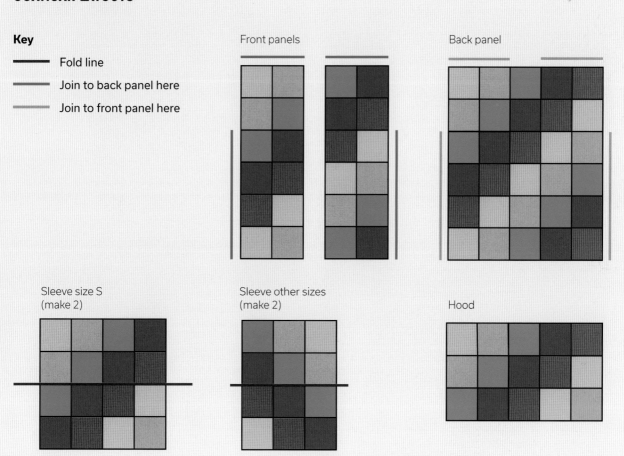

Key

— Fold line

— Join to back panel here

— Join to front panel here

Front panels

Back panel

Sleeve size S (make 2)

Sleeve other sizes (make 2)

Hood

97

3. Create your granny squares

Make 101 for XS/S, 93 for all other sizes.

All sizes:

Referring to the colourway charts work your granny square as follows:

Using first colour, 4 ch, sl st to first chain to make a ring.

Round 1: 3 ch, work 11 dc in the ring, sl st to third of 3-ch, fasten off (12 sts).

Round 2: join new colour in any gap between 2 sts, in the same gap work (3 ch, 1 dc), 1 ch, *in the next gap work 2dccl, 1 ch**, rep from * to ** all the way around, sl st to first dc (skipping over the 3-ch), fasten off (12 x groups of 2dccl, 12 x 1-ch sps).

Round 3: join new colour in any 1-ch sp, in the same sp work (3 ch, 2 dc), work 3 dc in every 1-ch sp around, sl st to third of 3-ch, fasten off (12 x groups of 3 dc).

Round 4: join new colour in any gap between groups of 3 dc, in same place work (3 ch, 3 dc), work 4 dc in every gap around, sl st to third of 3-ch, fasten off (12 x groups of 4 dc).

Round 1

Round 2

Round 3

Round 4

You will now shape the circle into a square.

Round 5: using yarn A, join in any gap between two groups of 4 dc, in same gap work (4 ch, 2 tr, 2 ch, 3 tr), 1 ch, work 3 dc in the next gap, 1 ch, work 3 dc in the next gap, 1 ch, *in next gap work (3 tr, 2 ch, 3 tr), 1 ch, work 3 dc in the next gap, 1 ch, work 3 dc in the next gap, 1 ch**, rep from * to ** twice more, sl st to fourth of 4-ch (4 x groups along each edge). Fasten off.

M/L:

Round 6: sl st in every st along to 2-ch sp, sl st in 2-ch sp, in same sp work (3 ch, 2 dc, 2 ch, 3 dc), 1 ch, work (3 dc, 1 ch) in every 1-ch sp along to corner, *in corner sp work (3 dc, 2 ch, 3 dc), 1 ch, work (3 dc, 1 ch) in every 1-ch sp along to corner**, rep from * to ** twice more, sl st to third of 3-ch (5 x groups of 3 dc along each edge). Fasten off.

XL/2XL:

Round 7: rep round 6 (6 x groups of 3 dc along each edge). Fasten off.

3XL/4XL:

Round 8: rep round 6 (7 x groups of 3 dc along each edge). Fasten off.

5XL/6XL:

Round 9: rep round 6 (8 x groups of 3 dc along each edge). Fasten off.

GRANNY SQUARE CHART

4. Assemble your coatigan

Holding two squares RS facing, using yarn A, join through two consecutive 2-ch corner sps on both squares, 1 ch, work 1 sc in the same sp, working through consecutive sts and sps on both squares work 1 sc in every st along, finishing with 1 sc in the 2-ch space, fasten off and weave in ends.

Join the squares into strips of squares first, then join the strips into panels.

Tip

Before assembling your coatigan, you may want to join the panels together with stitch markers first.

5. Join your coatigan

Use the sc join that you used to join the squares. Hold the two panels RS facing and work from the outside edge working through consecutive sts and sps on both panels.

Start by joining the shoulders, then join up the sides leaving two squares unjoined for the armholes. Fold the sleeves in half using fold line on diagram as a guide. Join the two sides together and join to body.

Three granny squares in the centre of the back and one on each front will remain unworked which the hood will be joined to (five granny squares in total).

JOIN THE HOOD TO THE BODY

With RS facing join the five granny squares at the bottom of the hood panel to the remaining five unjoined granny squares along the neckline of the garment. The bottom right granny square will be joined to the right front, the next three granny squares to the back of the coatigan and the fifth granny square will be joined to the left front. Now join across the hood seam at the top (working on the inside), see the pictures opposite.

6. Add the edging

BOTTOM RIB

You can choose to make your bottom rib deeper or narrower by adding more or fewer repeats of round 2.

Row 1: using yarn A, join in bottom corner, 3 ch, work 1 dc in every st and 2-ch sp along (153(189:225:261:297) sts).

Row 2: 3 ch, turn, *work 1 fpdc in next st, work 1 bpdc in following st**, rep from * to ** all the way around.

Rows 3–5: rep row 2.

Fasten off.

SLEEVE CUFF

For round 1 treat the ch sps as a st.

Round 1: using yarn A, join in any st at back of sleeve, 1 ch, sc2tog all the way around, sl st to first sc (34(42:50:58:60) sts).

Round 2: 3 ch, work 1 dc in every st around, sl st to third of 3-ch.

Round 3: 3 ch, *work 1 fpdc in next st, work 1 bpdc in following st**, rep from * to ** all the way around, sl st to third of 3-ch.

Rounds 4 and 5: rep round 3.

Fasten off.

FRONT AND HOOD RIB

Row 1: using yarn A, join on RS in bottom corner, 3 ch, work 1 dc in every st and ch sp up the edge, around the hood and back down the other side (316(388:442:532:604) sts).

Row 2: 3 ch, turn, *work 1 fpdc in next st, work 1 bpdc in following st**, rep from * to ** all the way around.

Rows 3–6: rep row 2.

Fasten off.

7. Finish your coatigan

If desired, sew on four toggle buttons as shown in the pictures.

Happy Sunflower
Cardigan

This is such a happy cardigan! Perfect for the spring and summer months or to brighten up a chilly day.

⊃ Materials

Wendy Supreme DK 8-ply/light worsted (DK), 100% acrylic, 3½oz/100g, 323yd/295m:

   2(2:2:2:2:2:2:2) balls in mocha (A)

   3(3:3:3:3:3:3:3) balls in sunshine (B)

   5(5:6:6:7:7:8:8) balls in cream (C)

⊃ Tools

4mm (UK 8, US 6) crochet hook

⊃ Gauge (tension)

Depending on the size you are making, your finished hexagon (edge to edge) should measure:

S: 4in (10cm) to end of round 4

M: 4¼in (11cm) to end of round 4

L: 4¾in (12cm) to end of round 5

XL: 5in (12.5cm) to end of round 5

2XL: 5½in (14cm) to end of round 5

3XL: 6in (15cm) to end of round 6

4XL: 6¼in (16cm) to end of round 6

5XL: 6¾in (17cm) to end of round 6

⊃ Pattern notes

The patterns in the book so far have used squares but these beautiful sunflowers are made into hexagons instead! They are joined together in one flat tessellation before being assembled into a cardigan. The length of the cardigan can easily be altered by adding more or fewer hexagons at the bottom of the cardigan.

1. Choose your size

Fit: loose

Size	S	M	L	XL
Actual chest circumference	28–35½in (71–90cm)	35¾–39¼in (91–100cm)	39¾–43¼in (101–110cm)	43¾–47¼in (111–120cm)
Finished chest circumference	39¼in (100cm)	43¼in (110cm)	47¼in (120cm)	51¼in (130cm)
Finished length	23½in (60cm)	25½in (65cm)	27½in (70cm)	30in (76cm)

Size	2XL	3XL	4XL	5XL
Actual chest circumference	47¾–51¼in (121–130cm)	51½–55in (131–140cm)	55½–59in (141–150cm)	59½–63in (151–160cm)
Finished chest circumference	55in (140cm)	59in (150cm)	63in (160cm)	67in (170cm)
Finished length	32¼in (82cm)	34¼in (87cm)	36½in (93cm)	38½in (98cm)

Louisa (right) wears the sunflower cardigan made in mocha (A), primrose (B) and eucalyptus (C).

2. Create your sunflower hexagons

Make 76 hexagons for the length specified in the size chart opposite. To make it shorter make 71, to make it longer make 82. You can also adjust the sleeves for length.

Always work on the RS.

All sizes work rounds 1–3, you will then follow the instructions for your size.

All sizes:

Using yarn A, 4 ch, sl st to first ch to make a ring.

Round 1: in the ring work 3 ch, 1 dc, 1 ch, *2dccl, ch 1**, rep from * to ** seven more times, sl st to top of first dc (skipping over the 3-ch), do not fasten off (9 x clusters including first 3-ch + 1 dc, 9 x 1-ch sps).

Round 2: in same place as sl st work (3 ch, 1 dc), in the next 1-ch sp work 2dccl, *in the next st work 2dccl, in the next 1-ch sp work 2dccl**, rep from * to ** all the way around, sl st to first dc (skipping over the 3-ch), fasten off (18 x clusters including first 3-ch + 1 dc).

Round 3: using yarn B, join in any gap between clusters, in the same space work (4 ch, 2trcl), 2 ch, *in the next gap between clusters work 3trcl, 2 ch**, rep from * to ** all the way around, sl st to top of first cluster (skipping 4-ch), fasten off (18 x clusters, 18 x 2-ch).

SUNFLOWER GRANNY SQUARE CHART

Symbol chart to show rounds 1–3 all sizes.

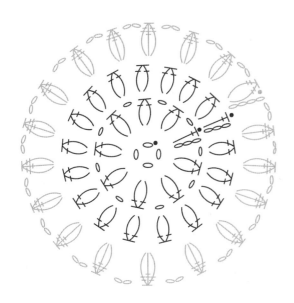

Rounds 1 and 2

Round 3

Round 4 (size M)

S:

Round 4: using yarn C, join in any 2-ch sp, in same sp work (2 ch, 2 hdc, 1 ch, 3 hdc), work 3 hdc in each of the next two 2-ch sps, *in the next sp work (3 hdc, 1 ch, 3 hdc), work 3 hdc in each of the next two 2-ch spaces**, rep from * to ** four more times, sl st to second of 2-ch, fasten off (12 sts along each edge).

M:

Round 4: using yarn C, join in any 2-ch sp, in same sp work (3 ch, 2 dc, 1 ch, 3 dc), work 3 dc in each of the next two 2-ch sps, *in the next sp work (3 dc, 1 ch, 3 dc), work 3 dc in each of the next two 2-ch sps**, rep from * to ** four more times, sl st to third of 3-ch, fasten off (12 sts along each edge).

L:

Work round 4 as for M but do not fasten off.

Round 5: 1 ch, work 1 sc in same place as sl st, work 1 sc in each of the next 2 sts, *in the 1-ch corner sp make (1 sc, 1 ch, 1 sc), work 1 sc in every st along to corner**, rep from * to ** five more times, sl st to first sc, fasten off (14 sts along each edge).

XL:

Work round 4 as for M but do not fasten off.

Round 5: 2 ch, work 1 hdc in each of the next 2 sts, *in the 1-ch corner sp work (1 hdc, 1 ch, 1 hdc), work 1 hdc in every st along to corner**, rep from * to ** five more times, sl st to second of 2-ch, fasten off (14 sts along each edge).

2XL:

Work round 4 as for M but do not fasten off.

Round 5: 3 ch, work 1 dc in each of the next 2 sts, *in the 1-ch corner sp work (1 dc, 1 ch, 1 dc), work 1 dc in every st along to corner**, rep from * to ** five more times, sl st to third of 3-ch, fasten off (14 sts along each edge).

3XL:

Work rounds 4 and 5 as for 2XL but do not fasten off.

Round 6: 1 ch, work 1 sc in same place as sl st, work 1 sc in each of the next 3 sts, *in the 1-ch corner sp work (1 sc, 1 ch, 1 sc), work 1 sc in every stitch along to corner**, rep from * to ** five more times, sl st to first sc, fasten off (16 sts along each edge).

4XL:

Work rounds 4 and 5 as for 2XL but do not fasten off.

Round 6: 2 ch, work 1 hdc in each of the next 3 sts, *in the 1-ch corner sp work (1 hdc, 1 ch, 1 hdc), work 1 hdc in every st along to corner**, rep from * to ** five more times, sl st to second of 2-ch, fasten off (16 sts along each edge).

5XL:

Work rounds 4 and 5 as for 2XL but do not fasten off.

Round 6: 3 ch, work 1 dc in each of the next 3 sts, *in the 1-ch corner sp work (1 dc, 1 ch, 1 dc), work 1 dc in every st along to corner**, rep from * to ** five more times, sl st to third of 3-ch, fasten off (16 sts along each edge).

3. Create your three-quarter sunflower hexagons

Make 2.

Using yarn A, 4 ch, sl st to first ch to make a ring.

Round 1: 3 ch, in the ring work 1 dc, 1 ch, *2dccl, 1 ch**, rep from * to ** five more times, do not fasten off (7 x clusters including first 3-ch + 1 dc, 7 x 1-ch sp).

Round 2: 3 ch (counts as part of first cluster), turn, in top of first cluster work 1 dc, *in the next 1-ch sp work 2dccl, in the next st work 2dccl**, rep from * to ** all the way along, fasten off (13 clusters including first 3-ch + 1 dc).

Round 3: using yarn B, on RS join in the top of the first cluster, 6 ch, *in the next gap between clusters work 3trcl, 2 ch**, rep from * to ** all the way along, work 1 tr in third of 3-ch, fasten off (12 x clusters 7 x 2-ch sps).

S:

Round 4: using yarn C, on RS join in 6-ch sp, in same sp work (2 ch, 2 hdc), work 3 hdc in each of the next two 2-ch sps, *in the next sp work (3 hdc, 1 ch, 3 hdc), work 3 hdc in each of the next two 2-ch sps**, rep from * to ** all the way around, work 3 hdc in the final ch sp, fasten off.

M:

Round 4: using yarn C, on RS join in 6-ch sp, in same sp work, (3 ch, 2 dc), work 3 dc in each of the next two 2-ch sps, *in the next sp work (3 dc, 1 ch, 3 dc), work 3 dc in each of the next two 2-ch sps**, rep from * to ** all the way around, work 3 dc in the final ch sp, fasten off.

L:

Work round 4 as for M but do not fasten off.

Round 5: 1 ch, turn, work 2 sc in st at base of 1-ch, work 1 sc every st along, *in the 1-ch corner sp work (1 sc, 1 ch, 1 sc], work 1 sc in every st along to corner **, rep from * to ** all the way around, fasten off.

XL:

Work round 4 as for M but do not fasten off.

Round 5: 2 ch, turn, work 1 hdc in st at base of 2-ch, work 1 hdc in every st along, *in the 1-ch corner sp work (1 hdc, 1 ch, 1 hdc), work 1 hdc in every st along to corner**, rep from * to ** all the way around, work 2 hdc in final st, fasten off.

Tip

For the shaped hexagons, from round 4 you will turn every round, so there is no need to slip stitch at the end of the round.

Three-quarter hexagon, size M.

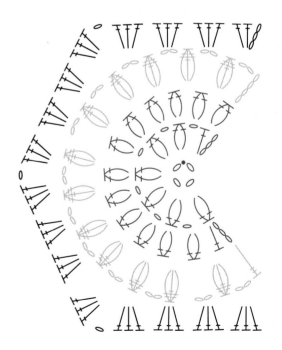

2XL:

Work round 4 as for M but do not fasten off.

Round 5: 3 ch, turn, work 1 dc in st at base of 3-ch, work 1 dc in every st along, *in the 1-ch corner sp work (1 dc, 1 ch, 1 dc), work 1 dc in every st along to corner**, rep from * to ** all the way around, sl st to third of 3-ch, work 2 dc in final st, fasten off.

3XL:

Work rounds 4 and 5 as for 2XL but do not fasten off.

Round 6: 1 ch, turn, work 2 sc in the st at the base of 1-ch and every st along, *in the 1-ch corner sp work (1 sc, 1 ch, 1 sc), work 1 sc in every st along to corner**, rep from * to ** all the way around, work 2 sc in final st, fasten off.

4XL:

Work rounds 4 and 5 as for 2XL but do not fasten off.

Round 6: 2 ch, turn, work 1 hdc in st at base of 2-ch and every st along, *in the 1-ch corner sp work (1 hdc, 1 ch, 1 hdc), work 1 hdc in every st along**, rep from * to ** all the way around, work 2 hdc in final st, fasten off.

5XL:

Work rounds 4 and 5 as for 2XL but do not fasten off.

Round 6: 3 ch, turn, work 1 dc in st at base of 3-ch, work 1 dc in every st along, *in the 1-ch corner sp work (1 dc, 1 ch, 1 dc), work 1 dc in every st along to corner**, rep from * to ** all the way around, work 2 dc in final st, fasten off.

4. Create your sunflower half hexagons

Make 7.

Using yarn A, 4 ch, sl st to first ch to make a ring.

Round 1: 3 ch (counts as a st), in the ring work 1 dc, 1 ch, *2dccl, 1 ch**, rep from * to ** three more times, do not fasten off (5 x clusters including first 3-ch + 1dc, 5 x 1-ch).

Round 2: 3 ch (counts as a st), turn, in top of first cluster work 1 dc, *in the next 1-ch sp work 2dccl, in the next st work 2dccl**, rep from * to ** all the way along, work two 2dccl in the final st, fasten off (10 x clusters including first 3-ch + 1dc).

Round 3: using yarn B and with RS facing, join in the top of the first cluster, 6 ch, *in the next gap between clusters work 2trcl, 2 ch**, rep from * to ** all the way around, make 1 tr in final st, fasten off (9 x clusters).

Now follow the instructions as for the three-quarter hexagons for your size (see page 107).

Half hexagon, size M.

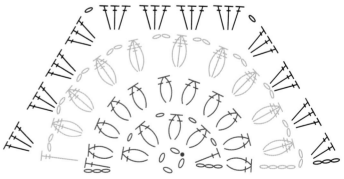

5. Create your sunflower triangles

Make 16 (2 of these are for under the arms).

Using yarn A, 4 ch, sl st to first ch to make a ring.

Round 1: 4 ch (counts as a st and 1-ch), in the ring work 1 dc, 1 ch, *2dccl, 1 ch**, rep from * to ** once more, work 1 dc, fasten off (3 x clusters including first 3-ch + 1 dc).

Round 2: using yarn B, on RS join in the third of 4-ch, 6 ch, in the gap between ch and dc work 2trcl, 2 ch, *in the next 1-ch sp work 3trcl, 2 ch**, rep from * to ** twice more, work 1 tr in final st, fasten off (4 x clusters).

S:

Round 3: using yarn C, on RS join in fourth of 6-ch, in same sp work (2 ch, 1 hdc), work 3 hdc in each of the next two 2-ch sps (the first being the remaining 2-ch from the 6-ch), in the next sp work (3 hdc, 1 ch, 3 hdc), work 3 hdc in each of the next two 2-ch sps, work 2 hdc in the final st, fasten off.

M:

Round 3: using yarn C, on RS join in fourth of 6-ch, in same sp, work (3 ch, 1 dc), work 3 dc in each of the next two 2-ch sp (the first being the remaining 2-ch from the 6-ch), in the next sp work (3 dc, 1 ch, 3 dc), work 3 dc in each of the next two 2-ch spaces, work 2 dc in the final st, fasten off.

L–5XL:

Follow instructions as for three-quarter hexagons, but picking up from round 5 onwards because there is no second row of clusters in the triangle, so no need for round 4.

Triangle, size M.

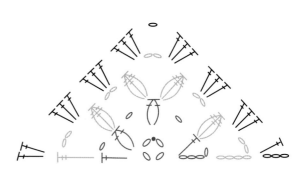

6. Assemble your cardigan

Assemble the cardigan according to the layout diagram below. Assemble into strips and then work down the strips to join them. Be particularly mindful of the under arm join where the triangle is joined. The hexagons are left unjoined on the three sides indicated in the chart then these three sides are attached to a triangle.

JOIN THE HEXAGONS

Hold two hexagons together with RS facing and using yarn C, join through two consecutive 1-ch corner sps on both hexagons, 1 ch, work 1 sc in the same sp, working through consecutive sts on both hexagons work 1 sc in every st along, finishing with 1 sc in the 1-ch sp, fasten off and weave in ends.

Join the other shapes in the same way.

CARDIGAN LAYOUT

Key

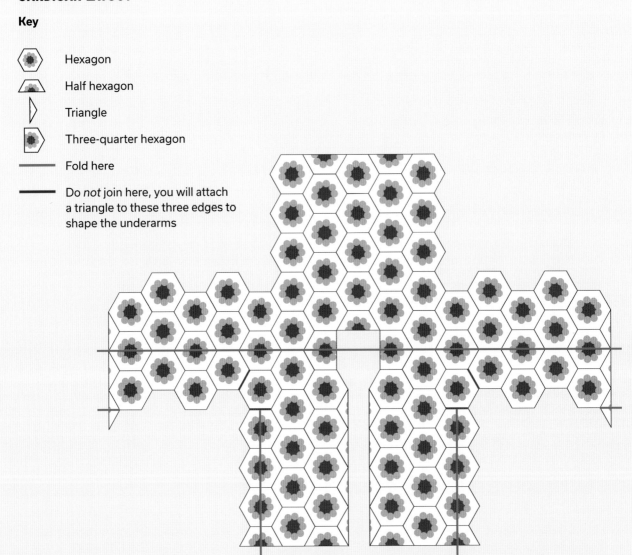

Hexagon

Half hexagon

Triangle

Three-quarter hexagon

Fold here

Do *not* join here, you will attach a triangle to these three edges to shape the underarms

7. Add the edging

BOTTOM RIB

Row 1: using yarn A, on RS join in bottom corner, 3 ch, work 1 dc in every st and 1-ch sp along, when you come to the half hexagons work into the ends of the rows working 1 dc in the end of the sc and hdc rows, 2 dc in the end of the dc rows, 3 dc in the ends of the tr row, 2 dc in cluster rows and 1 dc in 2-ch spaces.

Row 2: 3 ch, turn, *work 1 fpdc in next st, work 1 bpdc in following st**, rep from * to ** all the way around, sl st to third of 3-ch.

Rows 3–5: rep row 2.

FRONT AND NECK EDGING

Work from the bottom corner, up the edge, around the neck and back down the other side.

Row 1: using yarn A, on RS join in bottom corner, 3 ch, 1 dc in every st and ch sp along, when you come to the triangles work into the ends of the rows working 1 dc in sc and hdc, 2 dc in dc, 3 dc in tr, 2 dc in cluster, 1 dc in 2-ch sp.

Row 2: 3 ch, turn, *work 1 fpdc in next st, work 1 bpdc in following st**, rep from * to ** all the way around, sl st to third of 3-ch.

Row 3: 3 ch (counts as a st), turn, *work 1 bpdc in next st, work 1 fpdc in following st**, rep from * to ** all the way around, sl st to third of 3-ch.

SLEEVE CUFF

Round 1: using yarn A, on RS join in any st at back of sleeve, 3 ch, work 1 dc in every st and 1-ch sp along, when you come to the triangles work into the ends of the rows making 1 dc in sc and hdc, 2 dc in dc, 3 dc in tr sp, 2 dc in cluster, 1 dc in 2-ch sp, sl st to third of 3-ch.

Round 2: 3 ch, *work 1 fpdc in next stitch, work 1 bpdc in following stitch**, rep from * to ** all the way around, sl st to third of 3-ch.

Rounds 3–10: rep round 2.

Starry Night
Jumper

This is the perfect jumper for winter and would make a fabulous Christmas jumper!

➔ Materials

King Cole Glitz, 8-ply/light worsted (DK), 97% acrylic yarn/3% polyester, 3½oz/100g, 317yd/290m:

   3(3:3:3:3:3:3:3) balls in silver (A)

   6(7:7:8:8:9:9:10) balls in sapphire (B)

➔ Tools

4mm (US 6, UK 8) crochet hook

➔ Gauge (tension)

Depending on the size you are making, your finished hexagon (edge to edge) should measure:

S: 4in (10cm) to end of round 7

M: 4¼in (11cm) to end of round 7

L: 4¾in (12cm) to end of round 7

XL: 5in (12.5cm) to end of round 8

2XL: 5½in (14cm) to end of round 8

3XL: 6in (15cm) to end of round 8

4XL: 6¼in (16cm) to end of round 9

5XL: 6¾in (17cm) to end of round 9

➔ Pattern notes

Continuing the hexagon theme, these six-pointed stars are shaped into hexagons which are then joined to make your jumper. The length of the jumper can easily be altered by adding more or fewer hexagons at the bottom of the cardigan.

1. Choose your size

Fit: loose

Size	S	M	L	XL
Actual chest circumference	28–35½in (71–90cm)	35¾–39¼in (91–100cm)	39¾–43¼in (101–110cm)	43¾–47¼in (111–120cm)
Finished chest circumference	39¼in (100cm)	45¼in (115cm)	47¼in (120cm)	51¼in (130cm)
Finished length	23¼in (60cm)	25½in (65cm)	27½in (70cm)	30in (76cm)

Size	2XL	3XL	4XL	5XL
Actual chest circumference	47¾–51¼in (121–130cm)	51½–55in (131–140cm)	55½–59in (141–150cm)	59½–63in (151–160cm)
Finished chest circumference	55in (140cm)	59in (150cm)	63in (160cm)	67in (170cm)
Finished length	32¼in (82cm)	34¼in (87cm)	36½in (93cm)	38½in (98cm)

2. Create your star hexagons

Make 80 for the length specified in the size chart.
To make it shorter make 74, to make it longer make 86.
You can also adjust the sleeves for length. Always work on the right side.

All sizes work rounds 1–6, you will then follow the instructions for your size.

All sizes:

Using yarn A, 4 ch, sl st to first ch to make a ring.

Round 1: 1 ch, work 6 sc in the ring, sl st to first st, do not fasten off.

Round 2: 1 ch, work 2 sc in same place as sl st, work 2 sc in every st around, sl st to first st, do not fasten off (12 sts).

Round 3: 1 ch, work 1 sc in same place as sl st, *work 2 sc in next st, work 1 sc in the following sts**, rep from * to ** all the way around, make 2 sc in final st, sl st to first st, do not fasten off (18 sts).

Round 4: *6 ch, work 1 sc in second ch from hook, 1 hdc in next ch, 1 dc in following ch, 1 tr in each of the next two ch, skip 2 sts from round 3, sl st in next st**, rep from * to ** five more times, fasten off (6 points of star made).

Completed star.

Round 5: using yarn B join in any skipped 1-ch from round 4, *working down the edge of the point in the back loops of the sts, work 1 sc, 1 hdc, dc2tog, dc2tog across last stitch of this edge and first loop of next, continue to work up the edge of the next point, working dc2tog, 1 hdc, 1 sc, work 1 sc in skipped 1-ch loop at top of point**, rep from * to ** five more times, sl st to first st, do not fasten off (8 sts along each edge).

Round 6: 1 ch, work 1 sc in next st, *work 1 hdc in next st, 1 dc in following st, in next st work (1 dc, 1 ch, 1 dc), work 1 dc in next st, 1 hdc in following st, work 1 sc in each of the next 3 sts**, rep from * to ** five more times, on fifth repeat finish with 1 sc x 2, sl st to first st, do not fasten off (9 sts along each edge).

S:

Round 7: 1 ch, work 1 sc in same st, work 1 sc in every st along, *in 1-ch sp work (1 sc, 1 ch, 1 sc), work 1 sc in every st along**, rep from * to ** five more times, sl st to first st, fasten off (11 sts along each edge).

M:

Round 7: 2 ch, work 1 hdc in next st, work 1 hdc in every st along, *in 1-ch sp work (1 hdc, 1 ch, 1 hdc), work 1 hdc in every st along**, rep from * to ** five more times, sl st in second of 2-ch, fasten off (11 sts along each edge).

L:

Round 7: 3 ch, work 1 dc in next st, work 1 dc in every st along, *in 1-ch sp work (1 dc, 1 ch, 1 dc), work 1 dc in every st along**, rep from * to ** five more times, sl st in third of 3-ch, fasten off (11 sts along each edge).

XL:

Work round 7 as for L but do not fasten off.

Round 8: 1 ch, work 1 sc in same st, work 1 sc in every st along, *in 1-ch sp make (1 sc, 1 ch, 1 sc), work 1 sc in every st along**, rep from * to ** five more times, sl st to first st, fasten off, (13 sts along each edge).

2XL:

Work round 7 as for L but do not fasten off.

Round 8: 2 ch, work 1 hdc in next st, work 1 hdc in every st along, *in 1-ch sp make (1 hdc, 1 ch, 1 hdc), work 1 hdc in every st along**, rep from * to ** five more times, sl st in second of 2-ch, fasten off (13 sts along each edge).

3XL:

Work round 7 as for L but do not fasten off.

Round 8: 3 ch, work 1 dc in next st, work 1 dc in every st along, *in 1-ch sp make (1 dc, 1 ch, 1 dc), work 1 dc in every st along**, rep from * to ** five more times, sl st in third of 3-ch, fasten off (13 sts along each edge).

4XL:

Work rounds 7 and 8 as for 3XL but do not fasten off.

Round 9: 1 ch, work 1 sc in same st, work 1 sc in every st along, *in 1-ch sp make (1 sc, 1 ch, 1 sc), work 1 sc in every st along**, rep from * to ** five more times, sl st to first st, fasten off, (15 sts along each edge).

5XL:

Work rounds 7 and 8 as for 4XL but do not fasten off.

Round 9: 2 ch, work 1 hdc in next st, work 1 hdc in every st along, *in 1-ch sp work (1 hdc, 1 ch, 1 hdc), work 1 hdc in every st along**, rep from * to ** five more times, sl st in second of 2-ch, fasten off (15 sts along each edge).

3. Create your star three-quarter hexagons

Make 2.

For the shaped hexagons you will turn every round, so there's no need to slip stitch at the end of the round.

Using yarn A, 4 ch, sl st to first ch to make a ring.

Row 1: work 4 sc in the ring, do not fasten off.

Row 2: 1 ch, turn, work 2 sc in every st around, do not fasten off (8 sts).

Row 3: 1 ch, turn, *work 2 sc in next st, work 1 sc in following st**, rep from * to ** all the way around, do not fasten off (12 sts).

Row 4: turn, *6 ch, work 1 sc in second ch from hook, 1 hdc in next ch, 1 dc in following ch, 1 tr in each of the next two ch, skip two sts from round 3 (including the first st), sl st in next st**, rep from * to ** three more times, fasten off (4 points of star made).

Row 5: using yarn B join in the edge of the row before the bottom of the first point, 1 ch, starting your decrease in the same place and working up the edge of the point work dc2tog, dc2tog, 1 hdc, 1 sc, work 1 sc in skipped 1-ch loop at top of point, *working down the edge of the point in the back loops of the sts, work 1 sc, 1 hdc, dc2tog, dc2tog across last st of this edge and first loop of next, continue to work up the edge of the next point, working dc2tog, 1 hdc, 1 sc, work 1 sc in skipped 1-ch loop at top of point**, rep from * to ** until final point, working down the edge of the last point in the back loops of the sts, work 1 sc, 1 hdc, dc2tog, dc2tog across last stitch of this edge and the end of the next row, do not fasten off (8 sts along each edge).

Row 6: 3 ch, turn, *work 1 dc in the next st, work 1 hdc in the following st, work 1 sc in each of the next 3 sts (working around the end of the point), work 1 hdc in the following st, 1 dc in the next st, in the next st work (1 dc, 1 ch, 1 dc) **, rep from * to ** until final point, work 1 dc in the next st, work 1 hdc in the following st, work 1 sc in each of the next 3 sts (working around the end of the point), work 1 hdc, 1 dc, make 1 dc in final st.

Now follow the instructions for the whole hexagons (page 114) for your size but at the end of every row make a 1 ch and turn your work instead of sl st.

Three-quarter hexagon.

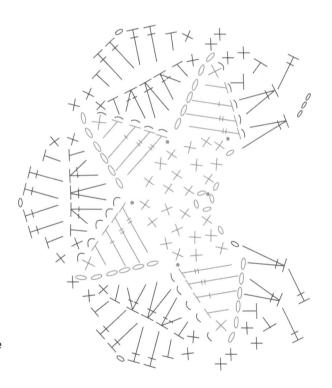

4. Create your star half hexagons

Make 8.

In yarn A ch 4, sl st to first ch to make a ring.

Round 1: work 3 sc in the ring, do not fasten off.

Round 2: 1 ch, turn, make 2 sc in every st around, do not fasten off (6 sts).

Round 3: 1 ch, turn, *make 2 sc in next st make 1 sc in following**, rep from * to ** all the way around, do not fasten off (9 sts).

Round 4: turn, *6 ch, make 1 sc in second ch from hook, 1 hdc in next ch, 1 dc in following ch, 1 tr in each of the next 2 ch, skip 2 sts from round 3 (including the first), sl st in next st**, rep from * to ** twice more, fasten off (3 points of star made).

Now follow the instructions for the three-quarter hexagons for your size.

Half hexagon.

5. Create your star triangles

Make 8 (2 of these are for under the arms).

Using yarn A, 4 ch, sl st to first ch to make a ring.

Row 1: work 3 ch in the ring, 2 dc, 2 ch, 3 dc.

Row 2: 3 ch, turn, work 2 dc in st at base of 3-ch, work 1 dc in every st along, in 2-ch sp work (2 dc, 2 ch, 2 dc), work 1 dc in every st along, work 3 dc in third of 3-ch (7 sts along each edge).

Row 3: rep row 2 (11 sts along each edge).

Fasten off here for S, M and L.

XL–3XL:

Row 4: 3 ch, turn, work 1 dc in st at base of 3-ch, work 1 dc in every st along, in 2-ch sp make (1 dc, 2 ch, 1 dc), work 1 dc in every st along, work 2 dc in third of 3-ch (13 sts along each edge).

4XL/5XL:

Row 4: 3 ch, turn, work 1 dc in st at base of 3-ch, work 1 dc in every st along, in 2-ch sp work (2 dc, 2 ch, 2 dc), work 1 dc in every st along, work 2 dc in third of 3-ch (15 sts along each edge).

Triangle.

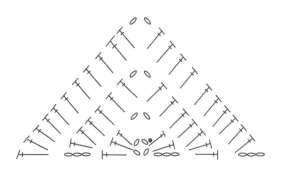

6. Assemble your jumper

Follow the layout chart below to assemble your jumper. Once it is assembled into a flat lay you can then fold across the fold lines and side edges and across shoulders. Please note the lines indicating where you do not join under the arm. Finish by joining a triangle to the three edges indicated on the chart for under the arm.

JUMPER LAYOUT

Key

 Hexagon

 Half hexagon

Triangle

 Three-quarter hexagon

——— Fold here

——— Do *not* join here, you will attach triangle to these three edges to shape underarm

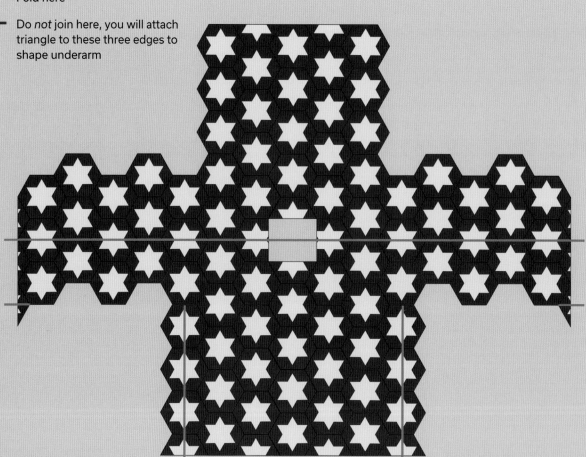

JOINING METHOD

Holding two hexagons RS facing, join B through two consecutive 1-ch corner sps on both hexagons, 1 ch, work 1 sc in the same sp, working through consecutive sts on both hexagons work 1 sc in every st along, finishing with 1 sc in the 1-ch sp, fasten off and weave in ends.

7. Add the edging

Work in the same way around the bottom, cuffs and neck. You can choose to make your edging deeper or narrower by adding more or fewer repeats of rounds 2 and 3.

Round 1: using yarn A, join in bottom corner, 3 ch, work 1 dc in every st and 2-ch sp along, when you come to the half hexagons work into the ends of the rows working 1 dc in the dc and hdc rows, 2 dc in the ends of the dc rows, sl st to third of 3-ch.

Round 2: 3 ch, *work 1 fpdc in next st, work 1 bpdc in following st**, rep from * to ** all the way around, sl st to third of 3-ch.

Rounds 3–5: rep round 3.

Louisa is wearing the star jumper made in King Cole Price Wise DK in admiral (main colour) with stars in silver, gold, azure and watermelon.

Tools and materials

On this page I have listed everything you will need to make all of the projects in the book. Your basic crochet tool kit for every project should include hooks, scissors, tape measure, a tapestry needle and stitch markers. For some of the projects I have used additional tools and fixings which you will find described here.

1. YARN

I have specified yarn brands for each of the projects in the book, but it is easy to make substitutions for different yarn or even to use your stash. See page 124 for more on this.

2. CROCHET HOOKS

I recommend a set of hooks with all sizes to hand so you can make adjustments for gauge (tension). For the projects in the book you will specifically need sizes 3mm (US 2/3, UK 11), 4mm (US 6, UK 8), 5mm (US 8, UK 6) and 6mm (US 10, UK 4), but please do read my advice on gauge (tension) in 'Secrets for success' on page 9.

3. SCISSORS

I like to use small embroidery scissors, but you could use any sharp pair.

4. NEEDLES

My preference is a darning needle for weaving in ends because it is sharp and has a large eye. To thread drawstring waistbands I used an aluminium wool needle, which has a plastic loop for the eye big enough to thread the crochet cord through.

5. STITCH MARKERS

Useful for marking stitches as specified in some of the projects, but can also be used to mark your place when counting the total number of stitches made.

6. TAPE MEASURE

For taking your body measurements and checking your gauge (tension) swatches.

7. BUTTONS AND TOGGLES

Toggles are used to fasten the Carefree Coatigan (page 94). Many of the cardigans in the book don't fasten, but you might like to sew on buttons as extra embellishments. I tend to source mine online, but any needlecraft store will also sell them.

8. BEADS

Used as optional finishings for drawstring waistbands and ties on several projects.

9. DUNGAREE FIXINGS

Used for the Woodstock Dungarees (page 36). These are readily available to buy online.

10. BAG HANDLES

Used for the Feel the Magic Bag (page 22). I used 6in (15cm) bamboo rings for my bag handles, which I sourced online, but you could get creative and add any handles you like, or reuse some another bag.

11. POMPOM MAKER

Used to make a fluffy pompom for the Winter's Day Hat (page 18).

12. BLOCKING BOARD

Used for blocking your granny squares to give them a neat, even finish. See page 9 for more on blocking.

Yarn substitutions

Throughout the book I have listed the yarn used for each project. I have used some of my favourite acrylic yarn ranges from Wendy, King Cole and Yarnsmiths (Wool Warehouse) as well as some pure wool from the Drops range and cotton from Drops, Cygnet and Scheepjes.

Although I have specified the yarn used in each project, it is very straightforward to make yarn substitutions. Lots of the projects in the book would look great made from your existing yarn stash!

If you would like to use a different yarn to the one specified in the project, there are a few golden rules which will help to ensure success:

1   The yarn you use must be the same weight as that for the project (i.e. fingering (4-ply), 8-ply (DK) and so on).
2   If possible use a yarn made from the same materials/ mix of materials, i.e. if made from an acrylic/cotton mix, look for a similar mix in your substituted yarn.
3   Check your gauge (tension) swatch is the correct size when made with the substituted yarn, and adjust your hook size if necessary.
4   When calculating the total amount of yarn used for the project, be guided by the length on each ball (i.e. the yardage/meterage). So if the project uses 10 x 3½oz (100g) balls of 100% acrylic yarn with 312yd/285m per ball, you will need a total of 3120yd/2850m of yarn for your project.

There are lots of ways to buy yarn. I would always recommend supporting your local high street yarn store if you have one. If not, there are plenty of good online stores stocking yarn and crochet supplies. My favourite is www.woolwarehouse.co.uk with worldwide shipping available.

Stitch glossary

Note that all patterns in the book are written using US crochet terminology.
Also see page 11 and the cover flap for the crochet chart symbols for each stitch.

US stitch	UK stitch	Stitch description
ch chain	**ch** chain	To make a chain, yoh, pull through loop.
sl st slip stitch	**sl st** slip stitch	Hook through st or sp, yoh, pull back through st or sp and through loop on hook.
sc single crochet	**dc** double crochet	Hook through st or sp, yoh, pull back through (2 loops on hook), yoh, pull through both loops.
hdc half double crochet	**htr** half treble crochet	Yoh, hook through st or sp, yoh, pull back through (3 loops on hook), yoh, pull through all 3 loops.
dc double crochet	**tr** treble crochet	Yoh, hook through st or sp, yoh, pull back through (3 loops on hook), yoh, pull through 2 (leaving 2 loops), yoh, pull through 2.
fpdc front post double crochet	**fptr** front post treble crochet	Yoh, from the front put hook under the post of the stitch, yoh, pull back through (3 loops on hook), yoh, pull through 2 (leaving 2 loops), yoh pull through 2.
bpdc back post double crochet	**bptr** back post treble crochet	Yoh, from behind the work put hook under the post of the stitch, yoh, pull back through (3 loops on hook), yoh, pull through 2 (leaving 2 loops), yoh, pull through 2.
tr treble crochet	**dtr** double treble crochet	Yoh twice, hook through st or sp, yoh, pull back through (4 loops on hook), yoh, pull through 2 (leaving 3 loops), yoh, pull through 2, (leaving 2 loops), yoh, pull through 2.
dtr double treble crochet	**trtr** triple treble crochet	Yoh three times, hook through st or sp, yoh, pull back through (5 loops on hook), yoh, pull through 2 (leaving 4 loops), yoh, pull through 2, (leaving 3 loops), yoh, pull through 2 (leaving 2 loops), yoh, pull through 2.
sc2tog single crochet 2 together	**dc2tog** double crochet 2 together	Hook through first st or sp, yoh, pull back through (2 loops on hook), hook through next st or sp, yoh, pull back through (3 loops on hook), yoh, pull through all 3.

US stitch	UK stitch	Stitch description
hdc3tog half double crochet 3 together	**htr3tog** half treble crochet 3 together	Yoh, hook through first st or sp, yoh, pull back through (3 loops), yoh, hook through next st or sp, yoh, pull back through (5 loops), yoh, hook through next st or sp, yoh, pull back through (7 loops), yoh, pull through all 7 loops.
dc2tog double crochet 2 together	**tr2tog** treble crochet 2 together	Yoh, hook through first st or sp, yoh, pull back through (3 loops), yoh, pull through 2 (leaving 2), yoh, hook through next st or sp, yoh, pull back through (4 loops), yoh, pull through 2 (leaving 3 loops), yoh, pull through all 3 loops.
2dccl 2 double crochet cluster	**2trcl** 2 treble crochet cluster	Yoh, hook through st or sp, yoh, pull back through (3 loops), yoh, pull through 2 (leaving 2), yoh, hook through same st or sp, yoh, pull back through (4 loops), yoh pull through 2 (leaving 3 loops), yoh, pull through all 3 loops.
3dccl 3 double crochet cluster	**3trcl** 3 treble crochet cluster	Yoh, hook through st or sp, yoh, pull back through (3 loops), yoh, pull through 2 (leaving 2), yoh, hook through same st or sp, yoh, pull back through (4 loops), yoh pull through 2 (leaving 3 loops), yoh, hook through same st or sp, yoh, pull back through (5 loops), yoh pull through 2 (leaving 4 loops), yoh, pull through all 4 loops.
2trcl 2 treble cluster	**2dtrcl** 2 double treble cluster	Yoh twice, hook through st or sp, yoh, pull back through (4 loops), yoh, pull through 2 (leaving 3), yoh, pull through 2 (leaving 2), yoh twice, hook through same st or sp, yoh, pull back through (5 loops), yoh, pull through 2 (leaving 4 loops), yoh pull through 2 (leaving 3 loops) yoh, pull through all 3 loops.
3trcl 3 treble cluster	**3dtrcl** 3 double treble cluster	Yoh twice, hook through st or sp, yoh, pull back through (4 loops), yoh, pull through 2 (leaving 3), yoh, pull through 2 (leaving 2), yoh twice, hook through same st or sp, yoh, pull back through (5 loops), yoh, pull through 2 (leaving 4), yoh, pull through 2 (leaving 3), yoh twice, hook through same st or sp, yoh, pull back through (6 loops), yoh, pull through 2 (leaving 5 loops), yoh, pull through 2 (leaving 4 loops), yoh, pull through all 4 loops.

Index

First published in 2025

Search Press Limited
Wellwood, North Farm Road,
Tunbridge Wells, Kent TN2 3DR

Text and patterns copyright © Sam Sabido, 2025

Photography
Photographs on pages 9, 10, 12–13, 16–17, 20, 21 (top),
24, 29, 33, 40–41, 48–49, 56–57, 75, 87, 88, 90, 98–99,
101, 105, 107, 108–109, 115, 116, 118–119, 123 and 124
by Mark Davison at Search Press Studios.

All other photographs and cover image by
Leanne Jade Photography.

Styling by Claire Montgomerie.

Photograph and design copyright © Search Press Ltd. 2025

ISBN: 978-1-80092-178-8
ebook ISBN: 978-1-80093-165-7

The Publishers and author can accept no responsibility for
any consequences arising from the information, advice or
instructions given in this publication.

Readers are permitted to reproduce any of the projects in
this book for their personal use, or for the purpose of selling
for charity, free of charge and without the prior permission
of the Publishers. Any use of the projects for commercial
purposes is not permitted without the prior permission of
the Publishers.

Suppliers
If you have difficulty in obtaining any of the materials and
equipment mentioned in this book, then please visit the
Search Press website for details of suppliers:
www.searchpress.com

Publishers' note
The book features the following models:
Louisa Roberts-West (see page 19)
Joy-Ann White (see page 15)
Emily Toledo (see page 31)

Bookmarked Hub
For further ideas and inspiration, and to join our free online
community, visit www.bookmarkedhub.com

About the author
See more from the author for further inspiration:
www.adventuresincrafting.co.uk
Instagram: @samsabidocrochets

Measurements
The projects in this book have been made using metric
measurements, and the imperial equivalents provided have
been calculated following standard conversion practices.
The imperial measurements are often rounded to the nearest
¼in for ease of use, except in rare circumstances; however, if
you need more exact measurements, there are a number of
excellent online converters that you can use. Always use either
metric or imperial measurements, not a combination of both.

US crochet terms
Note that all patterns in the book are written using
US crochet terminology. Some US terms for crochet
stitches differ from the UK system. For UK conversions,
please see the table on page 11, and there is also a handy
chart on the back cover flap that you can fold out to easily
refer to as you work.